You're Not for Everyone

A Soulful Guide to Authentic Living

By

Jackie Henderson

Written by Zinovia Canale

Dedication

To Faye Sotirakis,

My Teacher, Guru, and Guide

Thank you for instilling in me that my life is my own.

Table of Contents

Foreword 1

Meaningful Quote 3

Preface to: 4

Part One: Dreamer 7

   Chapter 1 - "My Father's Suicide" 9

   Chapter 2 - "Solo-Soul" 34

   Chapter 3 - "Mother-Daughter" 57

   Chapter 4 - "The Men" 85

   Chapter 5 - "Mother- Son Bond" 109

Part Two: Dancer 125

   Chapter 6 - "*Off the Curb*: Its Inception" 127

   Chapter 7 - "*Off the Curb* – Passion for Dance" 140

   Chapter 8 - "*Off the Curb*- The Power of a Mentor" 157

Part Three: Healer 177

   Chapter 9 - "More Past, Regrets, Relationships" 179

   Chapter 10 - "Manifesting Dreams" 198

   Chapter 11 - "Out of the Comfort Zone" 218

Part Four: Resources 235

    Resources for Chapter 1 - "My Father's Suicide" 237

    Resources for Chapter 2 "Solo-Soul" 240

    Resources for Chapter 3 - "Mother-Daughter" 242

    Resources for Chapter 4 - "The Men" 245

    Resources for Chapter 5 - "Mother-Son Bond" 249

    Resources for Chapter 6 - "*Off the Curb*: Its Inception" 253

    Resources for Chapter 7 - "*Off the Curb*- Passion for Dance" 256

    Resources for Chapter 8 - "*Off the Curb* – The Power of a Mentor" 259

    Resources for Chapter 9 - "More Past, Regrets, Relationships" 263

    Resources for Chapter 10 - "Manifesting Dreams" 266

    Resources for Chapter 11 - "Out of the Comfort Zone" 270

A Final Note 273

Works Recommended or Consulted 276

Foreword

By Zinovia Canale

I took this project on because I believe Jackie Henderson had a story to tell and I was excited to work with her to tell it. We began meeting in January of 2020 and have continued for over one year. In the beginning, I was not quite sure about where the story was going to go. I had my thoughts and of course Jackie had hers. Her story intrigued me, her words of wisdom helped me, and her beliefs and approach to life inspired me.

I knew of Jackie's work with *Off the Curb* and had the opportunity to attend some of the Dance Troupe's performances. I absolutely loved the artistry of the dance and thoroughly enjoyed the energy of the performances. I knew very little about hip-hop, but I had been involved in dance all of my life. Frankly, I was in awe of the hip-hop dance steps and moves, which was a complete contrast to the ballet I had learned. Many years later, I began taking Jackie's Cardio Dance and Physical Fitness classes and I thoroughly enjoyed her teaching style. She has a quick sense of humor, a whole lot of passion, and is an expert dancer.

A bonus of Jackie's talent is the belief in and practice of integrating the mind and body into her classes including Weight-Training, TRX, and Hip-Hop Step. We are always prompted to be mindful of our work while exercising. When she offered Mental Fitness, which later became Soul Fitness, workshops for self-exploration, I was enthusiastic to participate in those classes, which allowed me the opportunity to examine my own strengths and insecurities. I have participated in a number of self-improvement workshops, but none of them compared to the unique and sincere approach demonstrated by Jackie. She is authentic and compassionate, without placating to the fears or darkness of others. She does not mince words. She empowers individuals to assert themselves and to own their space.

Jackie Henderson has a gift for teaching and engaging those around her to strive for their personal best. As a certified Mental Health Counselor, it is easy to see how all of her attributes tie together. It is with all of her skills in mind that I approached the writing of her story, being attentive to her unique voice. It has not been an easy process in capturing her essence with all of its complexities and layers. But it has been a fulfilling journey, where I have become challenged to reflect on my own goals and desires. And that process has been an amazing revelation. Jackie Henderson is not for everyone, but she has been an inspirational person for me. I will always cherish and use the lessons she has taught.

I know that most readers will find wise affirmations, interesting observations, humorous anecdotes, and heart wrenching accounts within the pages of *You are Not for Everyone: A Soulful Guide to Authentic Living*. Those nuggets may inspire positive movements in your own lives, but for sure will prompt deep reflection. And deep reflection is always good for the soul. Happy reading.

For now she need not think of anybody. She could be herself, by herself. And that was what now she often felt the need of - to think; well not even to think. To be silent; to be alone. All the being and the doing, expansive, glittering, vocal, evaporated; and one shrunk, with a sense of solemnity, to being oneself, a wedge-shaped core of darkness, something invisible to others... and this self having shed its attachments was free for the strangest adventures.

Virginia Woolf -*To the Lighthouse*

Preface to:

You are Not for Everyone: A Soulful Guide to Authentic Living
"Why a Memoir and a Self-Help Book?"

Everyone has a story to tell and is worthy of telling it, although you may feel it is not important enough. I believe strongly that every person's story is important and holds information with which another person can relate. Not everyone wishes to reveal themselves and that is certainly an acceptable prerogative. However, I decided that now is a good time for me to tell my story for many different reasons. I have lots to offer to readers who are looking to become the best versions of themselves, and who want to read about an ordinary person who has had her brushes with fame. My book takes you on a journey through parts of my personal story with what I consider to be life lessons. Specifically, each chapter is structured to include a "Take-away" and a "Guidance" section based upon my personal experiences and my professional training. My training includes Dance, Physical Fitness, and Mental Health Counseling. A "Resource" section for each chapter is included in the last part of my book that corresponds in chronological order. The resource sections are narratives that explain why I have chosen specific books, videos, podcasts, and movies meant to be used as an enhancement to the messages conveyed. My book invites the reader to listen to what I have chosen to share about my experiences- how I found my voice, what I learned, and how I hope to help others. My wish for those who read my book is that they will take away helpful information that will guide them toward peace and happiness.

I realize that although I have been an inspiration for many people, I know I am not for everyone. The same is true for all individuals. As young children we have a natural inclination to want to be everybody's friend and perhaps as we grow older to be liked by all. But this is not realistic. We are not easily understood by all those we encounter nor are we liked or admired by all. This concept is important and necessary to acknowledge. The younger we learn to believe and trust in our own individual ability to honor our authentic selves, the better. Only then can we not give attention to the need to please or accommodate others and instead be open to receive the lessons the universe has to offer to each one of us.

My story is emotional, sometimes heartbreaking, and other times happy. It does not follow a chronological timeline and highlights what I have deemed to be insightful information to share. I have learned some valuable lessons that may impact others in a positive way. I am not interested in exposing my difficulties and conflicts for the sake of unloading my issues to relieve my insecurities, although that process does come a bit into play. I'm not speaking from an angry place to payback anyone. I'm a confident and successful adult who has weathered storms and lived a productive life. But I'm not finished. I have more to do and in this moment in time, I have cause to pause and reflect. Middle age is a good time to write about my life, the good and the bad of it, even though there is a natural resistance to share the darkest part of my soul. Middle age (I was born on March 8, 1967) is a natural milestone to scan the many chunks of time I have lived through and to evaluate what has occurred within those chunks.

I remain active both physically and mentally, and I embrace the aging process. I am a firm believer about the reverence, humility, and excitement that aging can entail. In spite of the obvious changes in appearance, and attitude, aging can be and should continue to be a vibrant process. All of the current research supports the behaviors associated with maintaining healthy nutrition, a consistent exercise program, and mental stimulation as a means to prevent in large part severe medical constraints.

My family is very important to me and is represented from a place of love, admiration and comfort. I have a wonderful son, who has been a constant light of my life. I have an older sister and brother whom I love very much. Our mother is an integral part of our lives and we are so grateful for all she has been to each of us. My siblings have both been blessed with wonderful families and I am grateful to have my nieces, nephews, brother-in-law, and sister-in-law in my world. As I write this memoir, I am curious and embrace the opportunity to reflect on my life to see what new discoveries exist as I look to my future. It is an exercise of the mind, body, soul, and spirit that I realize may disturb those close to me, which stirs up some anxiety in me. That makes me want to tread lightly. On the other hand, I want to be sincere, honest, and open with the most organic part of my being for the purpose of understanding my humanity. This is solely my story and I feel everyone has the right to undergo this exercise without having to screen their recollections as long as the telling is fair.

Part One

Dreamer

Chapter 1 - "My Father's Suicide"

Life becomes easier when you learn to accept the apology you never got.

Robert Brault

I was thirty-one when my father committed suicide. My father's final act lives in the catalog of my memories. His death was tragic, inexplicable, sad and changed me forever. It is sewn into the fabric of my life, but it does not control my future existence. Yet, I do acknowledge there is nothing worse in life than having to live through and absorb a loved one's suicide. Rape, murder, fighting in a war, and probably the most intense-losing a child are all horrific experiences that no one should ever have to endure. Against those tragedies, I suppose suicide would take second place. None-the-less, death leaves its survivors in a state of shock and with the harrowing revelation that there is absolutely nothing the survivors can do to alter the outcome. The finality is such a gruesome reality. No one is ever prepared to hear of the suicide of a loved one. The lone final act leaves the audience of family and friends forced into the challenge of coping emotionally, psychologically, and physically.

Initially, the pain hit me in my gut. The rawness of the cause of death filled buckets of tears, anxiety filled my nights, days lurked with a constant barrage of questions, while years were consumed with endless discussions trying to answer the proverbial "why?"

I have come to terms with my father's death as part of my life journey by becoming acquainted with myself on a deep level, exploring all that has contributed to making me the woman I am today. I have realized that although traumatized victims may not want to dig deep into the painful caverns of memories including how the body holds on to trauma, they must dig in order to fully understand its impact and to work toward healing. As a survivor and a grieving daughter, I knew I could not ignore my overwhelming feelings nor avoid the intensive self-analytical process necessary to get me back on my feet. I chose to do my processing under the guidance of a counselor who led me to lots of books about the grieving process and inner healing. I deeply longed to understand that which could never be fully understood. I needed help to figure out how I could push forward in spite of the confusion. Luckily, I had lots of support around me. My dancers demonstrated their compassion with thoughtful and simple acts of heartfelt caring gestures. Although they could never grasp the intensity of the complicated and deep sadness that I felt, they intuitively sensed my emotional distress. I had access to the professional services available through my program with the teens and I was able to call upon their expertise when necessary. My cousin with whom I had always been close stood by me,

Sharing the memory of the loss of my father brings the person he was back to me, as I think of who he actually was. Trying to encapsulate my father's essence is truly a mind and body exploration of both love and deep pain. So, with those thoughts in mind, allow me to describe my father. My father was very funny and had nicknames for everyone. I was "redhead" but also "tons of fun" because I would eat until I would fall asleep. My father taught us to never quit on anything. He encouraged us to join sports and to stay active since he had been a gymnast and an athlete who gained much value from those experiences. I followed somewhat in his footsteps although not as a gymnast. I was a dancer, I did cross-country, I did track, and I did lots of other sporting activities. He always came to watch everything I did, with pleasure and pride.

When I decided to give a series of apology talks, which I will describe in subsequent pages, one key concept I projected to my audiences was that I had perceived and considered my family to be a regular family. This whole thing of my father committing suicide was so outside our perspective and was never anywhere on my family's radar. Committing suicide would never have been seen as an option from the way I and the rest of my family knew my father. He never displayed or communicated any suicidal behaviors or statements. He was never really depressed. He was a little erratic at the end of his life because of his gambling addiction, which of course we knew nothing about until after his death. Our family rituals were similar to all those families around us. We always had dinner at five o'clock and sat around the table as most other normal families did during this time period. After dinner we wouldn't do anything unusual. We would watch TV, complete our homework, and then prepare for bedtime. Our family did not have many intense or engaging philosophical conversations, but once again that was the norm for most families. The father worked, the family had dinner together, the children participated in various activities and life proceeded with little involvement between the parents and the children. My parents were nice enough to each other and didn't have fights that we observed. However, I do remember one fight and it scared me because it was out of the ordinary. I cannot pinpoint what it was about. It was loud and they were screaming and I do remember being frightened because I had never heard such loud voices from them.

Unfortunately, my father was a womanizer which is difficult for me to face and talk about. I actually caught my father cheating on my mother. I was driving back home from an errand that I had completed and decided to stop by my parent's house which was in Bristol, RI at the time. There I found him with another woman. My parents were living in Bristol because my father had become the Chief of Police there following his retirement from the State Police. I must admit I was freaked out and I fled home. At home I was in the process of telling my husband (I was married at that point and divorced later) about what had just happened and all of a sudden, I looked in the doorway and there was my father. He was in a panic and had followed me home. I can only describe the scene as being bizarre. He wouldn't stop talking because he was as freaked out as me. This encounter was the only other time I saw him as erratic as he had been at the end of his life, speaking gibberish and in a panic. Neither of us knew what to do. I never told my mother, so nobody knows about this affair except for my ex-husband. I decided not to tell for two reasons. The first was because of a bible verse that states, "Love covers a multitude of sins." (Peter 4:8) I sincerely felt it was my role to protect my father. The second reason was, I just would not have been believed since my thoughts had often been dismissed. I hesitated in including the affair incident in my story because a part of me wanted to keep the secret as if I had never seen anything. My parents' pattern was to deflect problems and this is why I presume my mother would never have believed me. Witnessing my father's indiscretion was also very traumatizing.

In 1993, I recall my father was brought up on charges of sexual harassment. It was right at the same time Michael Jackson was going to court for the first time for his alleged sexual abuse charges. My mother was so mean about Michael Jackson (tried and convicted him before the courts even had a chance) and anyone who knows me knows what a diehard fan I am of Michael Jackson. I was being non-judgmental about the accusations against him until the facts were substantiated. On the other hand, my mother completely bought into the accusations against Michal Jackson and found him guilty without even waiting for the verdict. Conversely, she totally believed my father was innocent without even considering the fact that he may have been guilty. In my mind, I challenged her by saying, "How are you going to judge Michael Jackson who you don't know, and not judge your husband who you do know?" I could never say such a thing aloud. I did not have my voice at this point in my life. She had an idea about his philandering since at one point she asked him to leave the home. That stuck in my brain along with my father's behavior which remains solid in my memory. My father probably had affairs, seems like a manifestation of the times, men with their macho behaviors. This of course does not excuse his choices, but does place it into a context, albeit a disturbing one. I actually went to work with him one day and witnessed first-hand machismo behaviors. All the guys were swearing and talking how guys spoke in those days and I was mortified. My father never swore at home in front of his family and he was definitely a different person in the home than he was at work.

In his role as a detective, I saw that he was quite skilled. Certainly, his past molded him in a way that helped to hone his investigative qualities. I learned much about my father's childhood after his death because he never shared it with us growing up. In my search to attempt to comprehend what brought him to such a hopeless place, I became an investigator of sorts myself. And as I became older and further pursued my studies in the field of psychology and counseling, I was introduced to many inspirational thinkers. These thinkers helped me sort through the internal conversations I was having as we all have and to make sense as to how those conversations impact us. In so many instances, and in particular my father's, I concluded, "Who am I to judge or criticize you? How am I to know what you lived through and went through?" These sentiments were expressed by Wayne Dyer an American self-help and spiritual author who was also a motivational speaker and someone whose views I greatly respect. Still I was curious. When he was young, my father's family was super poor living and growing up in the South Philly projects. He moved to Rhode Island from Philadelphia after serving in the Marines and he never looked back. He was closest to his brother George and felt the need to be his overseer. In my apology talks, I called my father a "Robin Hood," stealing from the rich to give to the poor. On one occasion he stole a cake out of a bakery and ran it home to his brother George so he could have some semblance of a birthday celebration. Being so poor, inconsiderate people often made fun of the family which I assume left deep pangs of hurt within my father's psyche. The hurtful remarks may have motivated him to become an achiever, although the intense discomfort persisted in gnawing at him throughout his life. He was really good at his job because I think he understood the criminal mind. My father walked the line as a child, not that he was a serial criminal but he was a seasoned street kid. This expertise trained him in how to investigate and manipulate people to get at the truth.

On that fateful day, November 20, 1998 I was getting ready to meet my mother since she and I were supposed to meet my father for lunch. I was home alone in Saunderstown where my husband, our son and my mother-in-law lived at the time. I was in the midst of my routine, showering, figuring out what to wear, not at all expecting that in a split second my world would change forever. The phone rang and it was my sister who told me to sit down. I sat down and she broke the horrific news that an officer from Central Falls had called to tell her that our father had committed suicide. At that time my father was the Chief of Police in Central Falls following his position in Bristol. My immediate response in a matter of fact tone was, "That's an awful thing to say. Why would someone say something like that?" My mind could not absorb the severity of her words. I thought she was conveying some kind of gossip or a rumor.

It could not have been true. But she asserted calmly, "They're not saying it Jackie. It's true. He did that."

It took me a second to wrap my head around her words as the shock set in.

My sister then directed me with, "You need to get to mom. You need to tell her first before the police get there. You have to get there now!"

"OK." I answered and got off the phone bursting into tears. I ran upstairs and collapsed. I tried to get dressed but my legs wouldn't work. I stayed on the floor crying my eyes out and I called my husband. He couldn't understand a word I was saying. When he finally understood he came to the house and he drove me to my mother's house, and I knocked on the door and as she answered the door she said, "What's wrong Jackie? What's going on?"

I answered, "Tell me you know."

"Know what?"

"Tell me you know!"

Know what?" she repeated.

With that, I told her.

"Why Jackie? Why?" she asked with desperation.

And we both sat on the stairs and cried. Within the hour the whole house was filled with people. Lots of people just felt impelled to surround us with their support. Police, friends of my father, and family members appeared. My husband called my brother to tell him the awful news. My brother immediately got in the car and drove up from Virginia. I remember that moment in time becoming a chaotic scene with lots of people in shock, lots of tears, and lots of confusion. That evening we had an *Off the Curb* (the dance troupe I created which is described in great detail later in the book) performance scheduled and I figured I would just cancel it. Instead, my cousin relayed the horrible news to the kids who were all just devastated to say the least. But, to their credit, the performance went on. I spent the day and evening at my mom's house. The next day we had to shop for coffins, which was bizarre and surreal. I was operating from some robotic place and had to go to Marshals to get my mother an outfit to wear to a funeral- again, another surreal experience. We had three wakes because hundreds of people came. The funeral ceremony resembled the annual Newport Police Parade because the whole Central Falls Police Department marched down Broadway, the main street that runs through the center of Newport, RI. This is the usual route of the parade, except that this procession ended at the church and was led by a hearse. When we arrived to Saint Joseph's Church every step of the church was covered with police chiefs, fire chiefs, and many dignitaries, including Patrick Kennedy. All of the news channels were situated across the street. My father's death was statewide news. Wall to wall people were packed into the church for the funeral. It was a spectacular hero's send off. It was all beautiful and well done. I think I was in shock and numb the whole time. And we still didn't know why it happened.

When a policeman commits suicide the state police must investigate. We found out a few days after the funeral that my father had a gambling addiction and he was hundreds of thousands of dollars in debt. He had allegedly taken some money from the evidence fund from Central Falls as reported by an officer. My father was going to be brought up on ethics charges which was what one of his friends told him the Thursday evening before his suicide. My father couldn't live knowing that he would be disgraced…or so we assumed. My father couldn't live with that scourge on his soul and reputation so the next morning he killed himself. He had taken everything personal out of his police car. Anything that had to do with home, he simply separated it from his work belongings. He drove to the Central Falls station and killed himself in the garage. Most likely, one of the officers found him after they heard the gunshot. It makes me sad to think of him alone in that car having made that decision. I know it had to have been an extraordinarily tough decision. I'm saddened that he had found himself in such a desperate place. I wish he could have had a chance to pause but obviously not everyone has coping skills. I wish that I could have helped him knowing all that I know now after studying psychology as well as the work of spiritual leaders who have taught me so much. Pema Chodron is a Buddhist teacher, author and nun who practices the skills of peaceful living in turbulent times. She has written much but words that touched me deeply while I struggled to understand my father's suicide are: "If it were all glory, just one success after another, we'd get extremely arrogant and completely out of touch with human suffering." I wish my father could have known that we all would have stood by him no matter what the problem and that together we could have found a solution to his suffering. Chodron continues, "On the other hand, if it were all wretchedness and we never had any insights, and never experienced joy or inspiration, then we'd get so discouraged that we'd give up." He just must have felt so helpless and could not find the balance as explained by Chodron, "So, what's needed is balance. But as a species, we tend to overemphasize the wretchedness." It seems as if he just could not see a way out of his dilemma in spite of knowing his world was rich with family and friends. I don't think he realized the pain his act would leave behind. Instead, he thought he was helping everybody including his family and his co-workers. He saw this as his reasonable solution and in his mindset, it was the right thing to do. He lost hope, and focused on the wretchedness.

I think suicide is a very different kind of death because not only does it affect the surviving family members but it also carries a stigma. Individuals who have lost people tragically in a car accident or a murder or an incurable illness have the sense that the tragedy took their person away. They lost their person because of a concrete and unavoidable circumstance. My person did it on purpose and not everyone understands that. Unfortunately, there is a taboo that may be transferred on to the family, as if it was the family's fault. I just tend to not pay attention to judgments voiced by individuals who know nothing about the experience of being a first-hand suicide survivor. People make their own decisions and there is no stopping anybody from thinking and believing the thoughts that they have. My father was not the type of person who was hospitalized for depression or suicidal ideation. He never had that medical history, not that he ever displayed to us or his co-workers. His suicide was completely out of left field. Not one of us in my family had any inkling that my father considered suicide as a viable option for anything that may have been troubling him. The shock of his suicide definitely jolted my nervous system which took a long time and lots of work for my nervous system to reset. The shock to the nervous system was my mind recalling that my father put a bullet in his head and killed himself. My body definitely collapsed both hearing the news and years later. My whole body reacted as if it was hit by a freight train emotionally dispensing an earthquake of sensors throughout. Everything he taught me dissipated into thin air. He was the person who taught me to never give up, to always work hard, and that anything was possible. The week before he died he came to my *Off the Curb* office probably for the first time. While there he looked at all my pictures on the wall and the many clippings from newspaper articles. These artifacts were evidence of all that I had accomplished working with the kids who came from a wide range of environments some very challenging. He told me in a contemplative tone to both support and advise me, "Tell your kids if they need someone to look up to, tell them to look up to me because if I can make it out of the projects, then they can make it anywhere." He repeated, "If I can make it out of the projects and live my life the way I did, then they can do it too." I was touched that he took the time to visit and that he spoke so honestly and caringly. I felt as if he validated my work and that felt good. Yet, that was the week before he died. And so of course I couldn't tell that story. It had a bad ending. It was shocking. Everything he taught me, I doubted after that. Emotionally, on some deep level I was just shaken, my whole body was agitated. My belief system was shaken, my nervous system was shaken. His suicide was so out of the blue. I was so scared. What else was going to come out of the blue? I was emotionally scarred, very deeply. I found myself very empathic and sensitive to the slightest sad event. Thank God for my child because he forced me to stay healthy and keep going. I did end up staying at my mother's house for the week because I didn't want her to have to be alone. I took two weeks off from work to recover to the point that I could semi-function. It would have been far easier and far more appealing to simply escape into the darkness and live there for a while. But I knew I had to keep going for my child and my work. That meant I had to gather my strength to move on and live.

Understand, moving on does not mean that life continues as it once was. Instead moving on is at the primordial level, the barest ability to function. When you have that type of loss anything you felt before and anything you experienced before is no longer the same. Your new perspective is purely tenuous in every sense of the word. Everything you ever knew or believed is challenged and is second-guessed. You enter into a nether zone of your entire being. Trying to explain the depth of pain is virtually impossible because the pain consumes your physicality, your mind, and your soul.

I developed a deeper understanding that I could no longer take anything for granted. I think that the loss of a loved one by suicide will either make the survivor close up and withdraw or eventually allow the survivor to grow wider and deeper. I chose to grow deeper and let this feeling sit. It (the feeling) takes on a life of its own and needs the space to develop within your soul as an entity, as part of your own being until you can somehow come to terms with it. The "It" really consumed me and when I went back to work it was really hard to function in the present with the "It" circulating inside. I was very dark and would be there for a while. Nine years later I joined a grief group. Twelve years later I initiated the apology talks, titled *The Apology I never Got* as borrowed from the quote at the start of this chapter. The purpose for the apology talks was that I wanted a silver lining and I needed desperately to work toward healing. I wanted, too, as a result of this deep experience and pain to find the good in it. I strongly believed there had to be some good in it. The good was to help other people through the tragedy and heartache associated with the long haul to the new normal. It was also very cathartic for me because when my father died I closed the vault on my memories with him. I shut myself off from him out of a mixture of anger, disbelief, betrayal, and sadness. When I started preparing for these talks I was reminded of the happy times and how he lived up until the end. I could honor his life but also work through the sadness of his death. It was actually very helpful for me. I held the talks for four years for anybody who wanted to come and listen. Most people had been through a very deep loss and at least half were probably suicide deaths. Some were drug overdoses and some were tragic accidents. Those attending were in the throes of overcoming a tragedy. I always had about fifteen people in each sitting and the talks always allowed for deep sharing within a very healing atmosphere. I stopped the talks eventually because I was finished and ready to stop. Between my therapist and I, we conceded that I was healed for this period of time. I didn't have to keep running the groups and it was not necessary for me to keep telling the story. There was a reason that I was compelled to hold these sessions. Every time I held a session there was a specific group of people who needed to hear my story and to share their stories as well. I did it for the groups of people who needed to hear my tragedy to help them toward their own healing and then I was done. Currently, I will conduct grief groups as I see the need.

In my day to day life after my father's suicide, I must say I appreciated the people who acknowledged my father's death because I knew how awkward it could be. There were actually people who ignored it, and on the surface, pretended as if nothing ever happened to me. The truth is, my father dying did happen to me. I know intellectually these individuals said nothing because they did not know what to say and therefore avoided and ignored it. And for some of these individuals, I did lose respect for them because they could have at least struggled to find some comforting words to say since there is no question that my face was covered in grief. This was and is (still to some extent) my reality so I didn't want to be avoided for fear of bringing my father's death up in conversation. At the time, this was my life. Recovering from the shock and grieving the loss was what I was living. From my sadness and struggle to survive, I discerned that this is why I can talk so freely with people who have had deep losses because I know they want to be able to talk about losing their loved one and not pretend that nothing has happened. They know the loss is real like the "It" I had living inside of me, they are living with their own huge intrusion inside of them. If I ignore that intrusion and not honor it with my attention, then I am ignoring a huge part of them. When you are dealing with the death of a loved one often it seems like you are continually asked about how you are doing. I didn't mind the people who repeatedly asked me how I was. However, the questions did become exhausting after a while because it is nearly impossible to put into words a quick response and a concise update of the challenging work associated with building coping and survival skills for such a tragedy. On the other hand, having to answer, forced me to speak rather than just stand in silence. Gradually I moved toward a healthier place in my journey out of the darkness. Overall, I appreciated people speaking to me rather than ignoring what had happened. The story was reported in the paper and frankly, I didn't care about people gossiping. I can't control what people think about me. My life wasn't about gossip. It was about striving and moving forward. I was sort of insulated from hearing the gossip because I didn't care. I was too focused on what I was doing and hoping to accomplish so I didn't really let it affect me.

I would like to share a few words about my father's relationship with my son which makes me happy. My father was in love with my son. He called him "Monkey boy." That was his nickname. They had a special relationship as grandparents often do with their grandchildren. My son was only seven when my father passed away and he definitely was really sad. My son obviously was greatly impacted by his grandfather's death and expressed his feelings through a piece of his children's art. He had painted what I saw as a cute and colorful picture which traveled with me as I moved from various apartments. I always displayed the painting on the wall in each place I lived. But, I never really scrutinized the painting. I never realized the meaning behind this painting until one day after staring at it, the images and shapes, wondering, "What is this about" and it became apparent to me. They resembled guns. He had also drawn and painted a body with wings looking down and a body looking up from a prone position. The painting was clearly his way of processing and working through the loss of his grandfather. Perhaps, he needed to create a picture to understand in his own mind what he had heard to be true. In any case, I realized my son had "art therapied himself" for lack of a better term. For a number of years, I was traveling with this picture and it finally dawned on me. At one point, I was staying with my mom and it was my birthday and all of a sudden, my mother handed me a framed picture. She had taken my son's painting and had it framed, not knowing the significance of the piece. Yet she understood that it was important to me. It was a kind gesture on her part and she didn't even know how kind and how significant it was. It reinforces for me the power of the universe to intervene on our behalves.

The Take-Away:

I survived the darkness and had some profound take-aways as a result of my journey. I learned that tragedy and death are sacred ground. I have become a more compassionate person and continue to evolve in that capacity. I find myself reaching out to those who are dealing with death and grief with much more attentiveness, something, I may have been reluctant to do prior to my father's death. I certainly have developed a deeper sense of how fleeting life can be so I practice enjoying each moment as much as is humanly possible. I have learned it is unrealistic to believe that happiness can be prevalent in every day of every moment, which I think many people falsely believe. It is possible, however, to find the positive in each day and to relish it for a moment or gradual moments; and to make space to put aside struggles and allow peace in. It is a choice to honor the soul and body that work so hard for us every day. The body is so much more than a skeleton that holds us up and propels us forward. It can be a haven if we learn to listen to its signals- the pains, the discomforts, and ensuing illnesses- and address rather than hold onto them. The body harbors our myriad of traumas but will respond to our work to release the tightness and stress through our deep breathing and rigorous exercise all in coordination with using our brain power. I must have always ascribed my values to this truth because all of my life adventures have always led to the development of a strong body that has included exercise and one of the loves of my life, that being dance.

Guidance:

First, if you notice behavior changes in someone with whom you are close such as uncharacteristic erratic or out-of-character actions do not ignore these changes. Instead find a way to confront the person in a loving, calm, and serious way, to see if they are ok. Ask the questions. "Are you ok?" "Are you feeling depressed?" In some cases, you may consider broaching the uncomfortable topic of suicide by delicately and with sensitivity asking "Have you thought about hurting yourself?" For me, I do not think my father would have admitted that anything was going on. But at least I would have known I tried to reach out to him. That I tried to be there for him. My family all suspected that my father was going through something (nothing as extreme as suicidal thoughts). However, none of us confronted him to see exactly what was going on. And although our family was not one to discuss things openly, we were adults at that point and his behavior was very erratic so we should have known something was happening. But we just rationalized it away. In hindsight, we saw a red flag and brushed it aside thinking he'd be fine. Whatever his problem was he would take care of it. I cannot emphasize my suggestion enough. I repeat forcefully, if you observe extraordinarily different behaviors in a loved one, although it is uncomfortable and may feel that you are invading a person's privacy, speak to that person directly and push to have a loving conversation.

Second, if you do become a surviving family member of suicide, know that the healing work is intense and deep and you have to allow it to take its natural course. There is no time frame for healing. Just try and call on as many resources that you can such as:

participating in a grief group, speaking to friends or others that you feel comfortable with, reading books, listening to podcasts, finding any healthy outlet that will provide you respite from the sadness even for some period of time. I used a medium to help me connect to my father. I cried a lot. I was angry a lot. Know that you have to let the emotions be free and come out from the dark part of your soul. You have to feel the pain and you have to go through it to get to the other side of healing.

Third, use the painful experience as a catalyst to help others when you are ready. What I learned the day my father died was that most individuals embrace your loss and want to show sympathy toward you and your family through compassionate acts, like bringing food to your home, visiting, and verbalizing their condolences. Those gestures consoled us and made us want to do the same for others who subsequently had their own tragedies. None of us is ever immune from the deep sadness associated with death. We remembered the feelings of goodwill and reached out and talked and shared and comforted others as much as we could.

Fourth, when someone has a major loss in their life, don't avoid the conversation. That tragedy is first and foremost in the front of their mind, heart and soul and by avoiding any reference to the loved one's death is ignoring that person's existence. It is common for people to feel awkward or uncomfortable and they struggle to know what to say. But just acknowledging the death and loss is important because you are recognizing that irreversible alteration in someone's life. The survivor cannot perceive life again as s/he knew it prior to this death. It is not an exaggeration to say that when learning of a loved one's death, the survivor leaves his or her realm of reality to enter an alternative unchartered space. Recognition of the loved one, even a simple mention of his or her name helps the survivor to begin the grounding back from their dark place to a place that will hold hope for the future. Just saying, "I have no words" and offering condolences is an acknowledgment of their personal state of mind.

Finally, sometimes you don't even need words. Your presence is important by letting the survivor know you are there for them. Even if you don't know what to say, you can be there to sit with them in silence and provide a shoulder for them to lean on.

It is important to consider self-care practices when you have lost a loved one. The grief associated with death makes the surviving family members and friends literally lose their breath. Instead of breathing deep, strong, long, and healthy breaths, the breaths become small and shallow as survivors retreat inwardly feeling as if they have made themselves invisible. Immediately as any life trauma occurs, a difficult but healthy skill to learn is to become mindful about our breathing. We need to understand that inhaling and exhaling calmly is a means to relax our souls and oxygenate our organs. It is important to not drink alcohol or take drugs when grieving. Although they may numb you temporarily, they actually increase depression and sadness. Many people find it extraordinarily difficult to sleep but using relaxation techniques and breathing exercises to help you get enough sleep is crucial so your body can heal and mend itself in a healthy way. Adding some sort of support- a therapist, a grief counselor, and/or a friend/s that can listen and tolerate hearing you express your painful feelings is helpful. One's instinct may be to isolate, and perhaps for short moments that can be helpful… but certainly it is not healthy for long stretches of time.

Having an open and compassionate spiritual leader who can assist in connecting you spiritually without imposing judgements can be most helpful. We must remember however, that there are no "shoulds." For example, telling someone, "You should be over this by now" or "You should go to church" or "You should go out" is not productive. A person has to find their way back to their spiritual beliefs on their own terms in their own time because a tragic loss shakes all prior beliefs a person held before the death of your loved one. If you have a really true and compassionate leader, priest, pastor, or counselor they will have the innate understanding of the turmoil that grief creates and will help guide you rather than shaming you to feel a certain way. There are specific phases of grief but they do not happen in any particular order and they can happen differently for each person.

What often occurs after the death of a loved one is the redefining of family gatherings. In our family, we tried to maintain what we had before my father died, the holiday celebrations and other events, but it was too difficult. It became both obvious and painful that someone was missing. There was a protruding absence among the group of family members left with my father's passing. As extended family proceeded with their normal interactions, I sat back and thought, "How could you be laughing and joking?" Those thoughts circulated within me more prominently especially at the beginning when I realized the profound reality of the loss of my father. The effort to keep a sense of normalcy when things were no longer normal was excruciating. There does come a time when each person is ready to resume, "a new normal." But it is each family's individual choice to assume the task of creating new traditions and alternative methods of celebrating. There is not a clear outline or map to get to this spot. The task can be initiated by one family member or by a family discussion or with a little bit of both or it just evolves through a natural process. In my case, I couldn't keep going over to my cousin's home for certain holidays because it was too painful. It became a matter of coming up with new ways to celebrate with the question of, "What do we do now?" One option that seemed to develop organically in my circle was to have a holiday excursion with the women of the family and these trips brought us happiness and peace while still remembering our loved one. Essentially, our attempt was to turn the grief around into a happy occasion, knowing our loved one would not want us to continue to suffer. I would highly recommend shifting your thinking when and if you are ready to take the opportunity to explore finding new traditions as a family. Shifting the manner in which you think about finding happiness to bring the loved one's energy and presence into the celebration can be challenging but gratifying. Creating new methods, rather than trying to fit the old habits into a reality that no longer exists is a process.

Some individuals benefit from guidance in learning to conduct their lives differently as they face the changes that resulted from the death of their loved one. I have found in my practice that I can sometimes help my clients by reframing their thoughts or feelings or what they are experiencing. Sometimes through these sessions they discover that they hadn't thought of their predicament under those parameters. One outcome is they become more apt to try a new approach that may serve them well as opposed to remaining fixed in their distress. A grief counselor or a therapist who has been through similar circumstances can offer a client the understanding s/he may be seeking. Also, the benefits of participating in a grief group facilitated by a counselor who is familiar with the participants' circumstances can offer an individual ideas about how other people are dealing with their loss. You may be given a new perspective. It is important to note that healing does not happen until an individual is ready to take on the work.

I would like to offer additional thoughts and ideas to think about as you travel along the grieving road.

- Consider doing something to honor the life that has been lost.
- What would the action or symbol look like for you?
- Perhaps, light a candle with the person's name inscribed. Place it on a mantel or a special spot and light it for special occasions.
- Could you use artwork as an outlet?
- Could you maintain a journal of reflections, observations, or feelings?
- Have you ever thought about writing a letter to the person you have lost?
- Could you place a photograph or photographs in a specific place to speak to the person as if s/he were in the room with you?
- What feels right for you in honoring and remembering your loved one?

A final thought about my experience shared with me by a Reiki Master. I was encouraged to go to a place where my I had fun and good times with my father. Going to the cemetery, for me, was a reminder that my father was no longer physically present. But when I go to the blue rocks, a tiny park by the harbor where we had many relaxed and happy times as a family, I feel closer to him. Honoring the life of the loved one who has passed in the manner which feels right to you and brings you peace is the most important and appropriate ritual to keep, so that your loved one remains alive in your mind and spirit.

Chapter 2 - "Solo-Soul"

Though her soul requires seeing, the culture around her requires sightlessness. Though her soul wishes to speak its truth, she is pressured to be silent.

Clarissa Estes

What exactly is a solo-soul? As a young child, I felt alone. I was not sad and I had a spirit about me, playing and imagining like most happy and carefree children do. Yet, something was missing. I knew there was more to life than the banal existence I experienced, even though I could not articulate what the more was. I remember longing for attention from my family in terms of wanting them to validate my true self. Sometimes I felt as though I was living in an invisible body and wondered why they did not notice. I was caught between going through the rote actions of life that I thought everyone experienced, and the urge to share the constant stirrings of love within my heart that no one in my family could see or feel. We were the picture of a normal white middle class family, but like all families we had our not so pleasant histories that I think became subliminally infringed upon all of us. Our household consisted of my mother and father, my sister, my brother, and me. We lived with our maternal grandmother in her house, who managed the daily chores of the household. I never knew my maternal grandfather because he passed away when I was one. My grandmother certainly had her set of baggage that infiltrated the home through her relationship with my mother. Although this story is not about my mother's and grandmother's relationship, it is worth noting how their dynamic created a particularly tense atmosphere in the home. Certainly, there were other factors that contributed to the overall feeling in my home, which was sometimes a conflicted space. My grandmother was very responsible and took good care of us, available to tend to our basic needs. We all relied on her and loved her. She had her nightly ritual once we were all in bed which was to have her cocktail of choice to relax and end her day. I would not define her routine as problematic but none the less curious. My grandmother's life had not been easy, living with my grandfather who was depressed and dysfunctional. Much pressure was placed upon her to maintain her household and raise her children under those difficult circumstances, which without question affected my mother. As an unfortunate result, my mother and my grandmother brought a heavy aura into the home, with no conscious awareness of what they were doing. They did the best that they could and loved us (maybe not my grandmother toward my father), with no intentions of hurting anyone.

As a young, free-spirited child I had no words to articulate what I later understood as an adult. I operated on raw and instinctual emotions. I remember being a happy go lucky child that had a vivid imagination and a strong desire to be helpful to others and to please all those around me. I just do not recall sharing my stories or activities as they happened or having lots of playful conversations and games with my parents. There existed a distinct separation between child and adult. This was not a deliberate decision on their part to ignore me or my siblings, but rather their behavior toward us was a common pattern prevalent among most adults and children during this time. I, however, had a yearning to eliminate this gap. I wanted to be close to them. I wanted to be seen. When I think about my first memory, I can see how it laid the groundwork for both my strong will and my future ability to trust. That first recollection begins to form our core beliefs. It is the start of creating our own individual judgments, although we are not fully conscious of the importance of the impact until later in life when we can discuss and unpack the significance of life events. My first memory was an interaction with my father who took me to the park at the "Rich" as it is known to Newporter's but whose official name is Murphy Field. There at the park was a grand stone slide-built ages ago which still exists. I remember my father insisting that I slide down the slide. I was three years old and that slide looked daunting and frightening to me and I did not want to go down it. I vehemently objected, expressing myself as clearly as a three-year-old could by wailing "no" with crunched facial creases and mournful eyes. But my father vehemently insisted, assuring me that nothing bad would happen because he was there to take care of me. Needless to say, he won the battle and I slid down the slide. As I feared, I split my lip and blood dripped from my injury and tears rolled down my cheeks pouring out of my eyes. I think my father tried to console me but even at that young age, somewhere in my mind I did not want to let him. I can see how this became a theme in my life. I didn't want to share any disappointments or distresses with my family because I did not want them consoling me. I wanted to keep those feelings to myself. I knew I had been manipulated to do something I did not want to do and I was angry and retreated into my own world. Being coerced into sliding down the slide and then getting hurt demonstrated that it was going to be a challenge to trust men in my future, of course with no premonition of this at my young age. Reflecting back, I am sure my father must have felt terrible as most parents do when they mess up hundreds of times when raising their children. But I do believe many adults do not trust the minds of children enough to allow them the dignity of choice and thus to honor their own intuitions. Adults are usually compelled to impose their will on the young for a variety of reasons. My father was spending some alone time with me and trying to have a fun time, as millions of parents do with their children numerous times over the course of their childhood years. He just did not pick up on the intensity of the fear behind my protests (not hearing me) and instead followed his own desire to prove to me that the slide was going to be fun. Yet, I'm left with the bruise of that first memory. Yes, it could have been a lot worse, but that is insignificant because all young children's feelings have an acuteness to them when innocence is violated and their safety is betrayed, whether it is intentional or not. And since I did not feel that I was heard, I began to learn to stay silent.

Remembering and recounting my childhood memories is not for the purpose of judging or criticizing, but an attempt to understand my essence, and in order to do this I have no choice but to sort out the past. What did my upbringing teach me about life and myself?

Lots of families during the years of my childhood lived with grandparents or near them. So, my situation was not unusual. The system in our house was basically that my grandmother cooked, cleaned, and put us to bed. I felt my mother was always present, but not often engaged. She spent a great deal of time with her mother and when I asked her recently about what she actually did in terms of her daily routine while we were young children, her response was that she helped my grandmother with meal preparation. I just do not have a clear recollection of where she was in her interactions with me. I wished she could have been a more present and nurturing adult in my life. I truly craved her companionship, but her attention was elsewhere. My mother was involved in the activities that many women and mothers at that time participated. She belonged to a bowling league, took us shopping for clothes and performed other various motherly and wifely duties. She later became a nurse sometime during my teenage years and after my grandmother died. I think her presence /absence resulted from her own childhood and therefore did not separate out her personhood with those of her children. I never felt that she could see into my mind or soul anticipating my likes and desires. I think I was regarded as an extension of her and not an amazing unique individual that extended from she and my father. Our family life existed as a typical group of individuals that lived together under the same roof and had dinner every evening at five o'clock with a predictable recurring menu. For a good span of my childhood my father was a Detective in Scituate, Rhode Island and in this capacity brought guests home to dinner from time to time. We never spoke openly about the guests but we all knew they worked for my father as informants. In hindsight, when I think back to my childhood, I realize that my father crossed a boundary in bringing his work into the home. To some degree, interacting with criminals was normalized and most likely influenced me in my adult life. Specifically, I am tolerant of various different types of individuals, including criminals, because I learned from my home life that everyone deserved validation. My father believed in "second chances" but probably should have made that distinction in his work environment. This is because without an explanation, a child can become confused and perhaps this learned behavior was to my detriment in formulating relationships. It would have been interesting to know more about my father's work since he truly must have had some fascinating stories.

When I think about my childhood, there is nothing that stands out as particularly exciting or out of the ordinary. Like most other families of the time who all apparently had dinner at five, we played in our neighborhood, went to school and church, and participated in our various activities. Additionally, like most families before America's social and cultural revolution of the 60s and 70s took a foothold that disrupted the status quo, we didn't communicate openly about feelings or problems. I never recall discussing anything personal with my parents or siblings. My sister confided in me about her ups and downs, but I kept my life to myself. No one told me I couldn't speak, but I didn't have the courage to challenge the norm. It was so much more gratifying to remain in my imaginary world rather than to be ignored or unapproached. Our family appeared to be a typical middle-class unit living the lifestyle of every other middle-class family. We were the picture of a cohesive family. But we never really knew the underpinnings of what made each of us tick. In the vacuum of silence that permeated the structure of my home, so much internal conversation and dialogue transpired that was missed by the very people who should have known me the best. The same is true for me. I should have been the one who knew my family intimately. But I was the child. I was just learning from the role models and leaders in my environment. It wasn't my duty to teach something I knew nothing about. The young Jackie who lived in the house and fulfilled her role as the youngest child wished that she could have been made to feel special at times as well as to bounce ideas and thoughts around with her family members.

Living in my grandmother's house brought its set of circumstances that were not always pleasant, although the living conditions were convenient more so for my mother, than for my father. My grandmother made it abundantly clear that the house was hers and that things would be done her way. Her nightly routine included watching the TV shows she chose while she drank each evening until she went to bed, probably drunk. Her house was small and we all gathered together to watch the television or went upstairs around another TV if we did not want to watch her programs. My grandmother was rigid and stuck in her ways who made very little effort to bring about compromise. Though very religious, she actually brought dark energy into the environment. She had her positive attributes, like her interest in yoga and reflexology. She enjoyed reading her bible and listening to sermons by Billy Graham. Those attributes and interests should have brought some softness into the home, especially in her interactions with my father. My grandmother and father did not care for each other, and because of their mutual dislike there was constant tension emanating in the atmosphere. I did not witness any verbal arguments, but I could feel and sense the tension and discord. When things would get rough, my father would take us all to the Newport Motor Inn for a break away from the house. Some may even interpret this as respite from a difficult person, to put it mildly. At one point my sister did overhear a conversation where my father really wanted to move our family out. But that was not going to happen because of the strong connection between my mother and her mother. I cannot speak definitively, but there had to have been some control and power issues going on between the two of them. We were not a family who talked openly about difficult issues and so I never knew the complete details of this enmeshment- my mother's and grandmother's relationship, overlapping each other with little independence. Interestingly, although my life's work has been to dig deep into past memories and concerns, there is much I have been unable to uncover in my own past life. With regard to my father, the short of it is that, my father and grandmother did not care for each other and nothing was going to change that. When she died, I sensed my father's relief. I must admit I was glad that he did have some time to live without my grandmother in the house easing the tension that her constant presence caused.

Although my childhood was shrouded by tension and my quest to be seen, I believe I was born with an intuition and a drive that works through me. This drive makes me compassionate and motivated. I did things as a young child that in today's environment would be considered adult driven. Today's bragging parents would have loved me. I had a paper route at eleven years old and thought about using some of my earnings toward kind gestures. One of my stops was at an elderly housing complex and I felt empathy for those residents. I actually felt bad for them, probably because they were old and confined and as a young child I couldn't see beyond their elderly faces. I felt sorry for them never envisioning these individuals as having been young, vibrant, and active citizens in their communities. I wanted to do something I thought would be nice and to bring them some happiness, even if it was for a brief moment. With the help of my grandmother, I used my money to purchase carnations around Valentine's Day. I gave them to the residents in those homes by placing the flower on their individual newspaper that I had delivered to each of them. I was not a member of a club or a church group that organized a bunch of kids to do acts of kindness. The idea to use my money to offer a gift to others emerged from my brain and heart. I'm not saying I'm some kind of child prodigy who conceived miraculous accomplishments for the well-being of humanity, outside of the realm of all other kind and caring people. But, I will take credit for being humane because that's who I was and am and not because someone told me to be this way. It was a simple gesture that filled my heart. I did learn right from wrong from my parents who raised us all the best way they knew how. However, I'm not even sure if my parents knew that the elderly housing was on my paper route, not that they would have known the specifics of who comprised my paper route anyway. The point is, it would have meant much more to have shared my happiness and fulfillment with them instead of being invisible or unacknowledged.

Despite the fact that I lived in a household that did not encourage expressing emotions, my essence was one of happiness. I chose happiness. I would have to say I was not conscious at my young age that I made such a decision as compared to adults who learn about their power to choose as they mature. I simply was and am an optimist by nature. In my solitary world, the narratives I created were positive and hopeful. At one point in my young life, I fantasized that I would be whisked away by the band *Kiss* and accompany them on tour. I knew I was loved by my parents and family, but love can be funny and I think there is a difference between being loved and being nurtured. I do not remember being consoled and hugged as I experienced the tragic events that children feel. My goodness, when I was ten years old, Elvis Presley died and I was devastated. I cried my eyes out and I never remember being consoled or spoken to about my sadness. And as I got older and began middle school, I discovered how kids can be mean for a multitude of reasons. I along with just about everyone else in the world had those mean interactions. My positive attitude and happy essence were not always appreciated by the kids around me and instead they used my happy go lucky personality as a means to intimidate. On one such occasion in middle school an ugly threat was written on the door to the locker room to the gym reading, "Jackie Moffatt dies." Under current school regulations nationally, that statement would be a huge cause for concern and most assuredly be considered as an act of bullying. Yet, no adult took notice to attempt to get to the bottom of how that statement had appeared on that door. And I never felt confident in turning to an adult both in school or at home to share this incident and express the sad and fearful feelings raised by such a verbal attack. I was both mortified and embarrassed. Not to be dramatic, but I suffered in silence. Complete silence. I was not open to laying my woes at the feet of my elders. And as I look back, I must say I never received the message directly or indirectly to do so. Things just sort of happened. I suffered, and then they faded away like the passing of a day-first sunrise, then daylight, and then the fading of sunset to the evening dark sky. It was a piece of the humdrum existence of what was to be daily life probably like the lives of most of my friends and family. But oh my, the undercurrent of family life. The "what's not being said, the what's going on in each other's head," and the challenges of the interactions outside of home, that were not brought back to be discussed. How heavy is the weight of silence? Being quiet and invisible is not an easy task. So how outrageous was it? That not one teacher saw the defamation and threat about me and did nothing? That statement at the least, was extremely scary, all because of nothing and most likely irrational jealousy that girls are conditioned to assume. I was happy and cute and therefore not allowed to relish in that carefree spirit. Pema Chodron, someone I highly respect says, "the persons who cause you the greatest pain are your greatest teachers." I had no idea about such a profound statement in those adolescent years. But I did know then that I was horrified and that I still have the memory and that all I really looked for was someone to understand and help me get through the pain without being so alone.

The internal monologues that all individuals have going on in their heads originate from the moment a child learns the power of language. And for me, the thoughts and ideas that churned within allowed me the courage to try new things without the fear of failure. To say that not a drop of anxiety or a tinge of second guessing my choices never entered into my mind would not be true. However, I learned that I could quickly dismiss those emotions to charge forward. At fourteen I spotted a flyer advertising the Miss Rhode Island United Teenager contest. I glanced at it and I have no idea why, but on an impulse, I decided to try out and enter the competition. I won. As part of my winnings, I was afforded a trip to Hollywood, Hawaii, and Washington DC. Now understand, I grew up in the non-helicopter parent generation. My parents had barely an inkling that I was competing for this title until the actual competition. But once I won, it is sad to think that I was not able to embrace their energy to help me prepare for my journey and share in the excitement of it all. It was understood that I could handle the planning and the details. It was my thing and my parents had their responsibilities to deal with that did not include my accomplishment. Off I went by myself embracing the adventure. I met all sorts of famous people from popular TV series such as *The Facts of Life* and *Different Strokes* while many miles away from home. Being Miss Rhode Island United Teenager, to some extent, was a foreshadow of what was going to occur later in my life. I think the stage was set for the thrill associated with the art of performance and all of the glamour that goes along with it, though not the conventional form like movie star chic but rather contemporary stylish. I was not the type of person to follow the crowd or to settle for the ordinary. Early on, I willingly left my comfort zone and did not become embroiled in the opinions of others. I did not want to settle for the mundane and therefore walked my own walk, which doesn't mean I did not have my circle of friends. Think about it. In today's environment putting a fourteen-year-old child on a plane to travel cross country on her own may be considered something short of child neglect. So, the glamour enticed me, as any innocent child might be and I was enthralled that I was surrounded by famous actors that had previously been only seen on television. The thrill of standing in their company made me feel a bit famous as well. However, with regard to the competition aspect- the clothes and make-up I knew that was not me at all. Looking back, I chalk the Miss Rhode Island United Teenager experience as an interesting interlude in my younger years where I saw a challenge that appeared compelling and I went for it. Taking the risk reinforced my self-confidence and the traveling was a welcome bonus.

There is no question that developing into a mature and independent adult is a tumultuous journey filled with numerous twists and turns. Yet, it is how one navigates the process that can be both interesting and confusing. My way, was that I was born with the skill to withdraw inwardly where I could live in my imaginary world. That does not mean that I disassociated from the outside world and its people. In fact, quite the contrary is true. I am not a person who needs to be surrounded by people to live a happy and fulfilling life. Instead, I have the necessary social skills to thrive among groups as is evidenced by my work and career, though I do cherish my alone time. All of my endeavors originate from an internal energy where I create scenarios to implement. At a young age, I accessed this space in my brain which lessened my fears and allowed me the luxury to take risks. My inward life coupled with my imagination made me fearless because I created stories that brought me pleasure. An idea popped into my head and I tried it. If it worked, great. If it failed, then I created a different way to proceed. It is my inner consciousness and I had the power to select the characters, the colors, the scene, and the adventure. I experimented with the hindrances that I wished to overcome and decided my ending. I think I was lucky. I could have been depressed and negative because of how I felt invisible and as an unknown entity within my own family. Fortuitously, my imaginary world taught me at a very young age to cope with fears and failures while I had no clue that the universe was busy in guiding me in this direction.

Lastly, another simple episode that delineates my solo-soul is a time in my youth when I found myself sitting alone in church on one Sunday. When it came time for the sign of the peace during the mass, a young man sitting in the back of the church made his way towards me. He must have thought I was lonely and felt sorry for me. In any case, he approached me and gave me a hug and I was completely touched by his kindness because he noticed me. I had been seen by him and that simple act brought me true inner peace. That is a memory I carry with me that reinforces the need for all individuals to be visible to work toward becoming their best. I have realized that, "We are not prisoners of our past. We can retain control over how we decide to use aspects of our past in shaping who we want to be and become." (Batch)

The Take-Away:

What is the take-away of growing up in my household and recalling childhood memories, some happy and others not so happy? That I was a child left to fend for myself? Not really. That I was neglected? No. That no one cared? Not at all. The take-away is that I came to realize that self-reliance was understood. I had a life as everyone else in the family had. I was a student in school, no different than anyone else. No more or no less important. Everyone was responsible for figuring out their own concerns and issues. In my family, I never would have asked or expected to be hugged or consoled. Those jabs of pain hit the body and dent the soul, while also becoming a card in the catalog of the memory box stored deeply in the brain. There was love, maybe not the type of affection I longed for. My father showed us his love by honoring our birthdays and celebrating the holidays. He insisted that our birthdays had to be celebrated on the actual date, there was no waiting for when it may be convenient to celebrate. And for Christmas he wrapped the gifts. He meticulously creased the corners and made sure the packages were tightly and neatly wrapped. He would never think of using gift bags. That was the easy and lazy way out. He filled our stockings. My father, created and maintained scrapbooks for each of us chronicling our careers and achievements. He would come to our schools on Valentine's Day and bring us our own individual chocolates. All of his actions toward us, his children, were gestures of love and I am so grateful for those memories. I know now as an adult, that our childhoods imprint our souls resembling an oriental carpet with its scattered images of animals and designs, all symbolic of an act. That magic carpet holds you as you travel through life and is at the same time soft and comforting and rough and prickly. That ornamental and elaborate tapestry is the preparation for adulthood and does not disappear. Rather, the intricate patterns expand and gather layers once reaching the adult stage and moving toward senior hood.

Guidance:

It is important for parents to really see their children and for the children to feel that they are seen. Sometimes, our children are nothing like us and I'm sure every parent has had at least one moment where they look at their child and wonder, "Where did this kid come from?" It is absolutely imperative to accept children for who they are, even if they are entirely different from you. Parents may not always agree with the decisions their children make, but children have that right to charter their own courses, certainly with guidance. I was born during the "kids were seen and not heard from" era where parenting was understood to be more or less a sterile duty of control. Children had to figure things out on their own with little conversation about various options, fathers were not present at the births of their children, and mothers were regarded as the primary caretaker. I realize now that as a young child I was raised by parents that were a product of their times, yet that does not account entirely for my longing feelings to be seen and more importantly to be understood.

Some specific thoughts I believe to be true when assuming the role of a parent follow. If you are going to choose to have children they have to be just as important to you as your own life is. The children have to be right up there along with your own self-interests and goals. In fact, the children take the front seat to your needs until they can fend for themselves. Sometimes, this is a difficult concept to accept and causes much anxiety, especially if someone is unexpectedly placed into the role as a parent. However, even if one is prepared, there is no guarantee you will fully understand the commitment. To some extent a person who becomes a parent must be willing to put their dreams and desires on hold for a given period of time when and if necessary to ensure that an adult is fully present for their child or children.

Additionally, a person becoming a parent must do some self-examination. If you grew up in a home stricken with addiction for example, and you are now an adult trying to raise children you really have to do the emotional work to understand the effects left on you as you move into the parenting role. You may have to learn how to be affectionate, caring, and present. One of the aspects of adult children of a parent who struggled with addiction is that they know what they do not want their homes to be like. They don't want them to be volatile and unpredictable like the homes they had grown up in so they create this illusion of normalcy. But, they do not have the emotional tools to actually provide the emotional components that need to be present in healthy homes. If you are an adult child of a parent who struggled with addiction, I would encourage you to undergo therapy or counseling in order to learn and understand your emotions which would enable you to share and express healthy emotions with your children. Parents sometimes think that the illusion they create can dim underlying emotions. But children can always sense dishonesty or an insincere atmosphere, although they may not be able to articulate those feelings. Understanding yourself as a complete imperfect individual is a gift to your children, when you use the tools you have learned to accommodate for those imperfections. You are able to model and teach your children the tools you have incorporated into your life to cope with your own issues in an authentic and healthy manner. Children see, understand, and then practice appropriate problem- solving skills learned from those closest to them. They are able to gain confidence in their own ability to function in a healthy manner because it is a natural and organic process in a nurturing environment. I have referred to adult children of those suffering with addiction as an example of those who should seek therapy or counseling in order to develop healthy parenting skills, but there are many levels of dysfunction within homes from which adults have been raised. Those adults aware of the hardships they endured should be especially mindful about the effects of their upbringing when choosing to become parents.

As a parent, you have to know your children and not expect them to be what you have preconceived or imagined who they would become. Parents need to allow their children to be free spirited individuals with space and flexibility to develop into the best versions of themselves. If you have a creative child, do everything you can to provide them the means to explore their creativity. Talk to your child and ask them what they want and what they dream of, and ask who they would like to be someday. Know where and how they spend their time. Make time to play and be silly and have fun. Your children are people and you must respect them as people with their own thoughts and dreams. Naturally, you have to provide guidance and boundaries, two essential parental responsibilities that all children want and need, though they may resist at times. Children also should feel a sense of trust and comfort to be able to share with their parents the conflicts or disappointments which are inevitable truths of life. In my case, I didn't feel that I could authentically share my trials and tribulations with my family because I felt as though they couldn't handle the disruptions. I would rather just keep them to myself. That was a tough decision for a child to make. It was not a decision I made consciously. It was intrinsic learning that I believed and lived by my whole life. And you can read in my story that there are certain things that happened along the way that reinforced those decisions.

Today, the family structure has dramatically changed from years past. The Norman Rockwell painting of father, mother, two children and a dog faded as the new paradigm was born. Family structure is not as important as the people who build the structure to include love, attention, and attunement to each other in the home. Gay couples, single parents, and other configurations of family units will all contribute to the well-being of their children as long as the environment that is created is safe, loving, open, and responsible. Establishing a nurturing and accepting home atmosphere sounds like an obvious task as a parental duty. Unfortunately, it is not always easy because some adults are generally unaware that with every word and action they say or take, they are demonstrating to their children how they face and deal with problems. It is inevitable that children will have problems, and parents have to be fully available to assist them in handling the stress even if they are uncertain about the best way to proceed. Children are constant observers and soak in all that they see and hear and often need intimate and engaging conversations with their parents to unravel conflicts and make sense of their own perceptions. Many parents do not fully understand the necessity of balancing feminine and masculine traits in their children. As a society we have struggled to grant children the leniency to express their individual desires, emotions, and pursuits. Sometimes societal norms frown upon females assuming traditional masculine interests or criticize males who follow traditional female interests. No doubt, society has evolved but needs to go further in order to encourage children to feel all their emotions and to experiment with any interests that emerge within them. These interests should not be judged or discouraged. If allowed, I believe children will come to their own conclusions about what is best for them. By no means is this a simple process, but the complexities are necessary for reasonable growth and development.

There is an organic longing for human connection and touch in a healthy family. When a closeness has been cultivated in the home children feel the warmth. There is a reciprocity of love and affection and is a direct manifestation of how a person feels about him or herself. If you feel warm and loving inside, you will feel this toward others. If you have been taught affection and love as a child, that is the kind of person you will be. Not all, but most. If you haven't been taught love or affection as being necessary then it is difficult to share these feelings. However, there are exceptions. There always are. Some people are born sensitive and compassionate and even though they weren't taught how to express their affection, it is their essence. Many studies have been conducted to determine the importance of affection for healthy child development- all concluding the same results, a child needs affection to thrive. If you are an adult and you lost out on learning how to be affectionate, I would encourage therapy to figure out what is blocking this instinct. What made affectionate displays uncomfortable? What did you witness that made that unsafe?

Think about incorporating self-care practices into your daily life routine as a way to learn how to gain a comfort level for affection. Some suggestions are:

- Practice hugging hello and goodbye to those you care about.
- Practice loving yourself by doing those things that bring you pleasure.
- Take warm baths with soothing products.
- Take yourself out on a date.
- Sit in the sun or by the ocean or go to beautiful areas and enjoy nature.
- Do things that make you feel special and warm.

When you begin to develop warmth for yourself, this will start to overflow to other people.

Finally, a word about affirmations. Our brains follow neural pathways. If you grew up in a home where you were always getting criticized or not getting any feedback at all or experienced an abundance of pessimism, your neural pathways may become negative. Additionally, if you were around negative teachers or coaches sometimes their cruel words can be ingrained in your neural pathways. In order to reset our brains, we need to practice affirmations. Instead of hearing negative voices or our inner critics we must start practicing hearing positive affirmations such as, "I am good enough," "I am happy," "I am successful," and "I deserve everything I want." Starting to say those affirmations will re-fire the neurons in your brains and by continuing to say them on a daily basis will eventually develop neural pathways that lead you to positive thoughts instead of negative ones. This practice is as difficult as creating a new road in the Grand Canyon. Healing is everyday work. It is worth repeating that the guide toward healing should include the healthy habits of exercising, good nutrition, and training our minds to think positively. It is especially harder if you have been raised in an abusive home, but with time, patience, and guidance change is possible. Hopefully, younger adults reach the realization of their worth, if having experienced a troubling environment because it is easier for them to create new habits by virtue of their youth.

Chapter 3 - "Mother-Daughter"

Although mother-daughter relationships are often idealized in our minds, in reality, they are frequently complex and surprisingly complicated. They are also varied. There are cultural differences in how mothers and daughters relate to one another as we get older. Every relationship between mom and daughter changes over time, but they also take many different forms, even within the same culture or the same family.

Barth, 2019

I cannot write about myself without a discussion of my relationship with my mother and her formidable influence. But how difficult is it to be excruciatingly honest with such a private connection? It is human nature that children subconsciously expect to grow up with the ideal mother. This expectation is so unfair to all the mothers of the world, because no woman can ever achieve such a high order. All women bring both their baggage and their gifts to mothering, never quite knowing how the balance will transpire. I know for me, all I ever wanted and continue to want is for my mother to be connected to me. I want her unconditional love, which truthfully, I believe I have and probably have always had. But I am not sure she totally understands the depth of this craving nor has the willingness to pursue understanding it. The longing I have centers around the desire to be seen and heard for who I am and not for someone who my mother thinks I should be. I would love it if she were unencumbered by her own issues to understand me as a separate being from who she imagines me to be, even though I know I am a combination of our background and our genetic composition. As the youngest of the three children in our family, our relationship is good but strained at times for complicated reasons, but mostly because of my struggle to adequately explain this need without being dismissed or misunderstood. As I have previously described, our family did not openly communicate so it would not be a natural process to sit with my mother and talk about these yearning feelings, especially since I developed the habit of remaining withdrawn and private. The feelings, however, do emerge. They do not emerge directly but rather in indirect discussions about topics of interest not necessarily significant ones, more like every day small talk that can easily erupt into arbitrary arguments. Among the many arguments that children have with their parents over the course of their lives, my disagreements with my mother are usually because of the inability to have a back and forth calm dialogue. We virtually do not have conversations, but rather we have debates which implies that someone has to come out as the "right one," the victor. In my adult life, and with all that I have studied and learned, I have tried to be selective about my word choices, so that to the extent as is possible, I am heard clearly without ambiguity or with inciteful phrases. Most issues are about minor current event topics or interesting emerging subjects, that somehow touch my mother's underlying wounds that I have no way of resolving or for that matter truly understanding. I would suspect neither does she. I do not judge her for her actions because in my mind, I feel she never learned the art of deep conversation that is absent of emotional and reactive quips. I realize now that although our conversations may have to do with insignificant topics something deeper is going on. In the moments when my mother and I speak about controversial topics where our opinions differ, I find my emotions beginning to escalate to anger and frustration. I realize that the emotions that I feel are hurt and disappointment because my knowledge is not always respected and even more importantly, once again I feel I am just not being heard. Instead, we are in a vacuum and my mother is asserting herself to make her point of view matter with no presence of mind that I am an active participant in the conversation. She closes herself up and refuses to hear another word. Her defiance and rigidity are like a stubborn child who does not get her way and chooses to pout. I see this behavior as being emblematic of her own insecurities. I find myself becoming critical and I so wish that we could avoid entering into an emotionally laden argument about a topic that has nothing to do with our relationship. Instead, I wish we could transparently address what may be lurking beneath the surface of both our souls with honesty and authenticity despite the discomfort that may be evoked.

My mother is one of four children, the middle female of three girls with a younger brother. She considers herself to be a middle child and because of her birth order she feels she has suffered. The middle child is never old enough and often too young for, fill in the blanks as fitting. Some middle children may also develop a sense of always being left out as well as being in a constant state of competitiveness. My mother's upbringing was a bit challenging; living with her mother who struggled with raising four kids, running a business, and living with a depressed husband. This story is about me and not my mother's life but we are products of our parents and I think it is important to at least understand how her childhood influenced my life. She is a pessimist by nature, which is understandable when taking her background into consideration. That pessimism does run counter to my optimism which often causes frustration because my attitude is to see the good in the world, in people, and in situations as much as is possible. I have since come to understand that it must have been difficult to have her mother living with her and our family, preventing any real privacy for she and my father. And certainly, having my grandmother in charge of the home contributed to my perception of never feeling my mother as the dominant force in her own home. As a young child I did not consider my mother to be the nurturing type because she relied heavily on her mother to take care of us. I seldom cuddled with her. There was very little affection shared among family members. I have a memory of her cleaning the wax out of our ears with a bobby pin which when I think about it now, it makes me laugh. At the time it was an experience associated with fun with my mother because to humor me she would tell me "the wax story." The story was that as people cleaned their ears and took the wax out they would make candles with it because there was no electricity. It was a silly, tall tale but I enjoyed hearing it. I enjoyed the pleasant interaction that happened between my mother and I more than hearing the story itself and kept asking to hear the story so I could have more of those interactions.

I remember I couldn't really tell her anything, and I continue as an adult to hesitate about sharing my life with my mother and for that matter with many other people (another chapter). My circle is rather small. I suppose I had decided at a very young age to never talk about my life or any of the struggles I was going through. I just kept everything to myself. I decided early on that I was going to handle life on my own. As far as my mother goes, I never felt invited into her world to confide in her or to ask advice or to sort through problems. The actual distance that most kids kept from their parents during their younger years was not unusual, but I still was not one of those daughters who would run to her mother for the support or comfort I may have needed at a given moment. I was also reluctant to get close for fear of getting shut down or have my mother over react. As a young child my cousin and I were often silly and rambunctious as most children are. After all, children learn so much from their play time and from venturing into frivolous games and experiences. I wanted to show my mother one of our little escapades which was playing with applying make-up, which we discovered we were really bad at it. Instead of trying to use make-up to enhance our features we turned ourselves into clowns and found it hilariously funny. A childhood sense of humor. I asked my cousin if we should show our colorful faces to my mother and she firmly said "No!" She did not want to show her. I think because she knew that my mother's reaction would not be happy and endearing. When we did show my mother, she did not find it funny and instead reprimanded us telling us to wash the make-up off and go to my room. She reprimanded me for playing around with make-up which was probably messy and disturbing but such an innocent, playful childhood act that was silly and fun. Her response in general was to say, "Go back to your room and behave!" and not laugh or share in this childish humor. It is so interesting that this many years later, I remember the feelings associated with such an insignificant memory. But I think at the time, I was looking for some sort of attention from my mother that validated my zest for life and instead all I felt was, shut down. I was a child having fun. It was hurtful to not have my mother "play" with me. Every time I tried to be silly or funny or adventurous, I would get shutdown. I am sure she would not interpret this interaction as I did. Most likely she was oblivious to the effect of her reaction, never meaning to be hurtful, but just not in touch with my world.

I felt my mother's wrath another time, not a childhood antic, but a teenage venture into a drinking experimentation. I cannot say this time the wrath was somewhat warranted. I was fourteen and I went drinking with my friends and ended up getting sick, and I realized I hated the experience of teenage drinking. As friends at that age do, we wrote notes back and forth to each other and one in particular had to do with the drinking jaunt and how I hated it. I of course did not want my parents to get hold of this note so I took it and ripped it up into a million pieces. My mother found the one piece that had the word "drinking" on it and she became unnerved, almost having a panic attack. She was so overcome with emotion that I never wanted her to know anything ever again because she just seemed like she couldn't handle anything disruptive about my behavior. In my own thoughts I was thinking, "Relax mom. All teenagers experiment and I tried it and hated it. You do not have to jump from anger to uncontrollable panic." I was looking at her thinking her response was so over reactive. I could not believe she had not gone through similar encounters with my older siblings. It could have been that I was the baby that made her become so upset. Perhaps, the fact was that none of us ever really got caught doing terrible things. We always seemed like the perfect little kids. We all avoided getting caught for doing the things that teenagers do as they begin to grow into young adults and take risks. Meanwhile, we were sneaking out of the house at midnight to see *Rocky Horror Picture Show* after our parents were asleep. We knew what stairs to skip that squeaked We were not the perfect kids, just normal tumultuous teenagers. The fact that my mother was upset with me was reasonable, but the disproportionate reaction was disturbing and raised my anxiety. There was no opportunity to come back to the incident and discuss what had happened in a calm and close manner between mother and daughter. I was judged and convicted and there was to be no more mention of my behavior. This is how I felt and it reinforced my pattern to remain secretive about other incidences in my life, rather than take the chance of speaking up and provoking a similar reaction from my mother. She appeared more comfortable in not knowing details and I kept to myself for fear of having to feel her feelings of panic and fear. The truth of the statement written by F. Diane Barth, a psychotherapist who works with families and especially adolescents, "But how you communicate is extremely important. Accusing, attacking, and simply expressing disappointment is likely to keep you bogged down in a relationship stalemate" exemplifies a universal tenet of unhealthy communication skills. Instead, the fragile relationship between mother and daughter should be nurtured to include the idea that, "Expressing your feelings and making space for your mother or daughter to talk about her own can create a stronger connection." Maybe my mother just could not handle knowing about any behaviors that challenged her sheltered environment. Knowing what I know today after having raised a son, is that those adolescent years are so crucial to how a person develops as an adult. The groundwork is established and more than anything, adolescents need to have trusted adults around them. I am not suggesting that my mother was not a trusted adult. I am simply identifying the barrier she built between her own underlying issues and my need to be able to make mistakes, to talk about them, and to be guided to find the lesson from the person who is supposed to be the closest to me. I was never able to speak with her about the difficult times that included the bullying and mean girl affronts during my middle school years, where I would have surely benefited from a compassionate and loving ear. By the time I reached high school, I had become quite independent and therefore my pattern was firmly established- to rely upon my own internal resources to navigate through those years.

I know my mother is proud of me and my accomplishments. Watching as I pursue my entrepreneurial spirit by managing the many programs and activities I create, perhaps reminds her of her own past. I have created a multitude of performances as well as generated groups to use the many self-care practices I have studied. In addition, I maintain a physical fitness studio.

My work allows me a tremendous amount of freedom and creativity with lots of positive social interaction. The stresses of managing a business are not always so readily apparent. Obviously, my mother lived during a different time period and women were limited to where they could enter into the work force. Like a number of other women, she could not see beyond the stereotypical roles. My mother had lots of business ideas when she was younger but she didn't complete them because she didn't know how to and she didn't have the motivation. She just never followed through on the ideas that she had hoped to put into action. She has mentioned about how she never took any chances in her younger years as she observes me make my choices about my life and career. I know she supports my successes and wants me to be financially secure. I also know she enjoys participating in my dance classes and performing with the groups of women in the productions I create. But she doesn't fully understand or grasp the underlying practice or significance of my work, which is to create and develop all kinds of opportunities that support and uplift individuals or groups. I have a deep belief and value system that depends upon caring for humanity and assisting individuals to become the best versions of themselves. Oftentimes, I receive gifts like cards or my clientele extend themselves with kind gestures and my mother finds their admiration, respect, or generosity as something out of the ordinary. She actually asks," Why are they doing that for you?" confused about why an individual would display their gratitude towards me. I cannot surmise what is happening inside of my mother's thinking or what exactly is touched inside of her, but I would guess there are some underlying wounds. Addressing past wounds is a personal decision and can only be explored when and if a person is willing. I only know the impact I experience when asked a question such as the one my mother asked. And it makes me feel bad because it doesn't feel like she is sincerely sharing with me the positive emotions of fulfillment that I receive from my work. I would love her to be in alignment with the joy that parents attain as they see their children progress and reach individual goals. After all, I am her daughter.

Unfortunately, my mother's wounds are deep and I believe unexplored. As I described before, at times our emotions can clash. This again is not an attempt to analyze my mother or to recount her story but I mention it to explain the impact she has had on my life and the person I have become and continue to become. Her opinions are at times verbalized with rancor and I have to work hard to not allow myself to be brought "down" by the unnecessary negativity. I care deeply for my mother and I know she supports me and wants to help me and make sure I'm secure, but she just has a jarring bite that leaves me shaken. It is not unusual that parents allow their fears and judgements to enter into how they communicate with their children. And as far as my mother goes, there are three specific incidences where I was left feeling guilty, unsupported, or defeated by her words.

When I wanted to leave for California, my mother was very concerned about this decision making me feel as though I was abandoning her and the family. From my perspective, my leaving was to follow a desire I had to explore a new environment. I can understand her anxiety but I am certain the more constructive manner of dealing with one's emotions is to talk them through, something I desperately longed for with my mother. As soon as I got on the Newport Bridge on my way to California, I felt like I heard angels singing and a weight had been lifted. There had been no conversation between us, where my mother could logically point out her concerns. The non-conversation was simply a gut reaction on her part to impart her fears and lack of confidence on me while expecting the worst.

When I shared my decision to divorce my husband, the feelings expressed were similar, where I really could have used an understanding ear with helpful support. She didn't support me, listen to me, or give me permission to vent and express to her the issues that had brought my husband and I to the point of divorce. I think she had no idea that our relationship had gotten to this point, partly because I hesitated to share my personal life my mother. Perhaps my not preparing her for this drastic change justified her surprise, and may account for the harsh reaction she had expressed to me. But that did not give her permission to blame me for the break-up without having a deep and compassionate conversation with me.

Years later, as I decided to begin a private counseling practice my mother had her typical fearful reaction, when I could have used her belief in my skills and ability to make this move successful. I had worked hard to become a trained therapist, and her response indicated no confidence or faith in me. She did not recognize that to build a practice would take time and patience and I was willing to take this risk on.

My mother is not a villain for having the feelings she has and for expressing them to me. But I am like a sponge of sensitivity and continually wrestle with myself to not allow the negativity to take root in my being. I am not pessimistic by nature but I find sometimes that the inner critic in me assumes the form of the pessimistic person and I become sad or discouraged and must pull upon all of my coping mechanisms to resist the power of that voice. The message I was raised with was to play it safe, and that message is just not true to my nature and who I am. I must follow my heart and take risks that may or may not result in my preconceived notions. I cannot live any other way. I think my underlying personality traits are difficult to understand, especially if you are a person who hesitates in assuming challenges and has lots of fears about the unknown. It is nearly impossible to resolve the clash of wills between my mother and me.

Needless to say, after my father died our family struggled to find a solid footing, to begin to function, and to learn to enjoy life again without the perpetual cloud of darkness lurking above our heads, continually reminding us of the shocking horrific event. For my mother who has a recurring fear of being left out, this beginning leg of the journey was extremely challenging. The effects on the family following my father's suicide were devastating as we all in our own way swam through unchartered rough waters. My mother's pessimistic outlook on life had now been complicated with the added layer of overwhelming sadness. She had a really hard time traveling on her own. There was a big hole missing in her heart and she did not know how to fill it. She did not know how to gravitate warmly to her kids and grandkids. My father had this role and she was lost. We didn't quite understand this at the time because we were all figuring out how we would fill the holes in our own hearts. My mother was looking for all of us to reach out to her and to make sure we included her in our activities, to sooth her and to make her feel less alone. If we didn't follow through with these actions, she would shut down. But the complication was that we didn't realize that was how she was feeling because she was continually with one of us. The truth of the matter is, that only an individual person can find their way in their own time to begin to repair the damage left behind after such a tragic loss. It did not matter that she was with us physically, because emotionally she was alone. Her husband was not there and it was difficult for her to find her place in the family without my father's presence. This is what I believe after trying to makes sense of what my mother and our family experienced after the loss of our father and her husband. I can only express how badly I feel about her inability to recognize the caring and love surrounding her. I along with my siblings cannot repair the deep-seated wounds, trauma, or issues that reside within her. It is that longing that yanks me to want to make things better and to listen to her real concerns or pain. She always sees herself alone even though she spends much time with us and we would never exclude her. Nothing ever seemed or seems enough. I think the effect on me is that I continually attempt to fill her void either consciously or subconsciously, hoping to receive a different response or reaction. I know that the better way for me to proceed would be to let go and simply accept the emotional and psychological state in which my mom resides, and to remain focused on all of the positive things around me.

    I consider myself to be an affectionate person and I am curious about how this came to be. I never remember seeing my mother and her mother hugging or showing any affection toward each other, even though they were always together. I previously mentioned that I seldom cuddled with my mother, but my father would always give us a kiss good by when he would leave for work as part of his daily routine. Yet, I am a hugger and I encouraged and modeled this behavior with all of the *Off the Curb* kids in the spirit of being open and proud about caring for each other. As for my son, I completely smothered him with affection when he was a baby, and as a young boy I hugged and kissed him. We snuggled as most mothers and children do. We have a beautiful energy with one another that includes both affection and open communication. To this day as a grown man I hug him and he hugs me.

Because of my mother's background, she cannot relate to our relationship or doesn't quite understand how touching and hugging can be intimate without being sexual. When my son was twelve we took a road trip with my mother to Graceland. I dragged the poor kid there. At one point my young son and I cuddled together to watch a movie at the end of a busy day. My mother was just not accustomed to my interactions with my son and I could easily sense her discomfort with my display of affection toward him. My mother projected her feelings that my behavior was unnatural and that made me appalled and sad at the same time. Her perception said much about her mindset and I understood that our child-rearing methods were not at all the same. My mother's attitude toward touching, feeling, and displays of affection were learned behaviors present during her childhood which certainly must have been carried into our home. The energy in my house was heavy not only because of my father's and my grandmother's negative relationship, but also because there was no display of warmth. Love was not displayed with warm-hearted demonstrative gestures of hugging, kissing, or touching. Those gestures were subdued or attempted with awkwardness. My father did try to cuddle with me. But I didn't feel comfortable cuddling with him. I don't know exactly why. He had a weird energy that made me uncomfortable so I didn't want to be that physically close. My intuition led me to believe that he saw me as both his daughter and as an unrelated female. My father's attempts to get close was the nearest semblance to any affection that I was going to ever receive as a child. But it wasn't "cuddly, cuddly." The parental affection that children need is just as important to a child's development as the moral lessons taught to children in the home. When that piece is absent, something is absent in the soul and is a challenge to reconcile. Lessons are not learned only through language, but through actions as well. I think my mother never learned the beauty of pure affection. Or at some point she received a thwarted interpretation, and as such unintentionally transferred them on me (perhaps my siblings) or situations that touched that place of discomfort. When I look at my brother and his daughters, even as teenagers they climb all over him and sit on his lap and it's so sweet and it makes me feel happy. It's so pure. And I'm happy they have that intimacy. As I explained, I don't feel that I ever had that pure physical affection from my father and I do wonder what difference it would have had on me if I had felt it. It gratifies me to see my brother's interactions with his daughters because I know how important it is for children to feel the sheer pleasure of being fully loved. It's the same way when I'm with my son. It's pure love. There is nothing dirty about it. There is nothing weird about it. It's just beautiful.

My parent's relationship was interesting. They participated in attending our activities and events as dutiful parents. They loved one another in spite of the problems they may have had, which all marriages experience. My mother would sit with my father once he came home from work, after spending most of her days with my grandmother. As I got older and after my grandmother died, I recall my parents spending more time together. My mother went back to nursing school and I could see that she was beginning to follow through on her own individual life goals and desires. She obtained a position at Newport Hospital as a registered nurse after completing her schooling and training that she had begun as a younger woman, which I think was a brave move on her part. My mother was well respected in her position at the hospital and thoroughly enjoyed a long career. Her colleagues both enjoyed her and respected her skills. I think good nurses are very considerate, thoughtful, and thorough and my mother excelled in those qualities. Nurses are caring but they don't get attached. They're detached. My mother could perform exceptionally in that capacity. She loved going to work and I think it filled a huge gap that she had longed for but for whatever reason was unable to fulfill while her mother was alive. Toward the end of my father's life my parents spent lots of time going to jai alai (a sport played in a walled space with a hand-held wicker device which involved betting on the players). The Newport Jai Alai facility has since closed as its popularity waned in America. Gambling was a form of recreation that they enjoyed together. My mother still enjoys gambling, not visiting casinos but loving the thrill of betting on things, enjoying the competition, and especially winning. My parents were never affectionate in front of us except when my father would kiss my mother good-by. It totally made me feel uncomfortable. It was weird for my siblings as well. I would cover my ears. Their display of affection bothered me because their kissing did not appear as an endearing gesture, but more sexual in nature. My mother was never "love-y, dove-y" toward us so, when she kissed my father it felt uncomfortably sexual, rather than affectionate and I can still hear the sounds of their slurping, which frankly repulses me. Children in general never want to think of their parents as sexual beings, and perhaps that is what I was feeling. But as I reflect back, I think the quality of their interaction was somehow different. It was almost like I was brought into their sexual lives purposefully and I did not want to be there. I am positive my mother and father would never have seen it this way. The energy emitted had to have stemmed from both of their childhoods, having been raised during a time period when the topic of sexuality was hidden and ignored, unlike the sexual revolution that took hold later on in America.

When my father was alive, I considered their relationship as a husband and wife involved in some sort of play. My father assumed the role of the main character and my mother was the supporting actress. After my father died, it took my mother awhile to find herself and to find her voice, understandably. The new voice that emerged was very pessimistic, again understandably since her whole life had been shattered. She is still very wounded and hurt. In addition to losing her husband, she holds onto the fact that she was a middle child and neglected. My mother is convinced that every middle child is going to have a horrible life because they're all going to be neglected. Interestingly, although her mother lived with her and my mother spent much time with her, she never discussed those feelings with her. Unfortunately, childhood wounds cannot heal if they are not faced. It is like placing a band aid on a person who is bleeding to death, by making a blanket statement (like being neglected as a middle child even when you are not truly the middle sibling) to ease the feelings rather than explore the veracity of them. The band aid or the hug will not erase the severity of the problem. It's true that in the past, in many families it was not common practice to expend energy and time discussing issues. The expectation was to accept the cards that were dealt to you and move on, but the human psyche just does not work in that way. The issues will surface and the fears will never resolve themselves on their own.

My mother did seek solace through a grief group after my father's passing and that was a brave, helpful and a positive move on her part. She continues to maintain relationships with some of the participants. I think it has been a long, difficult road for her and after many years she has learned how to enjoy being with herself. Most people want to always be accepted by everyone, which is absolutely unrealistic. They do not understand that being with yourself can be satisfying, peaceful, and pleasurable and that individuals gravitate to certain other individuals for a variety of different reasons. It does not mean that one person is inferior to another. The choices lie within and depend much on one's own self-esteem. And although I do long for something different in my mother-daughter relationship, I can separate out those attributes about us that are quite satisfying and positive. My mother has a good relationship with my son and she and my father would babysit him when he was a baby and were integral persons in his life. My mother continues to be an integral part of his life. Even though I have described her as somewhat unaffectionate, that has not been an obvious quality to my son because it is part of his warm nature to hug his grandmother and to joke and laugh with her, and clearly, she accepts his warmth. I am very proud of how she evolved into her life after my father died. The shock of losing her husband by suicide is just so scathing. She had to have had strength to rebound from that tragedy. She found hobbies that she really enjoys. For a few years she wanted a partner and just focused on finding a companion. But now she has found contentment in living on her own. She keeps herself occupied with lots of activities. She loves to play golf. She loves to take photographs, and finally took the leap to sell them at the annual Holiday Party I hold for local artists, after years of my encouragement to do so. She helps her friends who are older and not as active as she is. She participates in attending my cardio dance classes a couple times a week. My mother has many interests and I am proud of her energy as a seasoned woman in her seventies. She took part in the *Women in Unity Performance* by dancing the Rosie Shuffle (one of my community productions) and truly enjoyed the full experience of the filming process with a positive attitude. She has also participated in other performances which I have produced. Our family makes it a priority to spend time together so celebrating birthdays and holidays are filled with meaningful traditions. I am proud of who she has become and what she has accomplished.

My mother and I shared a pretty amazing period in time when we visited a medium years ago. The day scheduled for the meeting happened to fall on my mother's birthday and I saw that as a sign to include her with my session. I was a bit apprehensive in having my mother join me because I had no idea how she would accept this experience. The first thing the medium started talking about was that angels appeared to her in the room with us. She saw me in a little dance outfit, dancing around the house. She said I wore a red bonnet.

To be noted when a medium is working with a person and their energies, they receive visions which is what our medium saw. The medium does not really know the meaning of what she is seeing. Only the person who is interpreting it fathoms the significance, which doubters may consider some sort of a scam. To me, the red bonnet was my red hair because my father used to call me "redhead" when I was little and I used to wear my little ballet outfits around the house and dance around in them. It seemed very real to me that my father's presence was with us in that session. The medium went on speaking, and shared things that made my mother and I feel really peaceful. She also told us that my father wanted us to know that when we see a butterfly, that represented him reaching out to us. Fascinatingly, my mother said she had just received a birthday card before she came to the session that was covered in butterflies. The things the medium spoke about really touched our lives and made a whole lot of sense to us. She subsequently asked us if we had any questions. My mother asked my father through the medium, "Why did you leave us?" and he responded, "I didn't leave you, I left myself." His answer just made us both cry. When the session was completed, we both felt very peaceful each in our own way, but together. I was happy that my mother was just as open as I to hearing the messages from beyond and hearing from my father, her husband.

The Take-Away:

My first take-away is to fully emphasize that I love my mother deeply. I have shared my emotions and thoughts in a guarded fashion, not meaning to hurt anyone. I think all people have different levels of dysfunction in their homes because, after all, there are no perfect families. I also believe that the level of dysfunction in the home does not matter to the child in terms of mitigating the longing that each child feels for their mother's love. It is human nature to have this instinct. Every child just wants their mother to be happy with them and continually seeks her approval. In my childhood home, I knew my grandmother was the nurturer and the person in charge of maintaining the running of the home. I'm not sure if there was ever any conversation about how the roles were determined but I lived under the conditions that were established and that became my normal. I knew in other homes the mother took on the duties that my grandmother had in my home, but as I said one gets accustomed to their own established pattern. As an adult woman and mother, I recognize how complicated relationships can be, especially between a mother and a daughter. I have realized how extraordinarily important it is for mothers to recognize that every child needs different things and that they see their children as individuals. Not all siblings experience the same feelings toward their parents, and in particular their mother. It is imperative that the mother know each of her children. She needs to know their likes and dislikes, their spirits, their souls and what makes them happy or sad. When a mother understands the unique temperaments of each of their children, then when the child displays a change in their personality, it is noticeable, even if the change is nuanced, the mother is present to assist, support, or comfort. Intervening during those difficult moments gives the child a sense of security and stability as well as laying the groundwork for developing a strong sense of self-confidence, creating emotional regulation, and building a healthy self-esteem.

During my childhood years, the common practice was to refrain from outwardly acknowledging the feelings of children. If there was a tragic event or death you didn't talk about it. The parents assumed that the kids would eventually "get over it." We have learned over time that that is not true. We now know that children are paying attention to everything around them. Parents having conversations with their children, even if it is about bad news is beneficial and necessary so the adults can help guide them through the uncertainty and painful emotions.

Another take-away is, once a couple has chosen marriage, in order to maintain a healthy partnership, the family dynamic has to shift to make each other the top priority. If the husband or wife does not come first, then a wedge may develop between them. At the very least, the union of the couple must be the entity whereby the rest of the family finds its connection. For whatever reason in my mother's case, that shift did not seem to happen and instead she relinquished her power of the household to her mother. I wished she could have moved out of her mother's home and had her own home with my father, while keeping a close relationship with her mother. During this time period, I am sure for convenience and financial considerations, it was not unusual to live with your parents. The difference is in how the couple establishes their parameters and that process is not always a clear-cut process. I think my mother became passive and submissive to her mother. There were times my father wanted to leave and I have to believe it was a dilemma for my mother, yet ultimately her mother's needs took precedence. The difficulty for my mother in separating from her mother certainly had an effect on our family unit, and for me I was left confused and disheartened. When my grandmother died I was well into my teens and then my mother turned to my father as the manager of the home. By that time, my pattern of keeping everything to myself was firmly established and I just did not have the skills to break through and request or demand to be seen and heard.

Once a pattern has been established in a family, it is difficult but not impossible to change it. And if you are a family member that does not necessarily follow the norms created by most other members, it is very easy to be judged and misunderstood. Because my family's communication was hindered and not a routine practice, I did not share my individual ideas, passions, and motivations with my mother. In that capacity, I appeared to be the "odd man out" choreographing hip-hop and building a business as opposed to entering a traditional profession like my parents and siblings. They may have thought my interest in dancing was admirable, but did not comprehend the day to day grind of the work nor the talent and creative aspects associated with the performance industry. I had the sense that my work was looked upon as a hobby or as some sort of outlet, rather than a full- fledged occupation. Often, parents believe they know what is best for their children, based upon their own perceptions, ideas, and desires. They tend to not empower their children to trust their own instincts. This can leave their children second-guessing themselves and resisting their independence. For me, I had a whole world percolating in my mind, body, and soul and I felt no one in my family could see that part of my spirit. I, therefore, had a feeling of being separated from my family. I felt they understood me from their own perceptions and how they wanted me to live the life they thought was best for me. But, I resolved, no, I'm finding my own voice and not falling in line. I had no choice but to follow my passion because of who I am. I decided to feed my soul. I think my family saw this separation as an unevolved reflection of who they were and could not give me due credit or acknowledgement of my spirit. My life choices are a reflection of who I am.

Guidance:

A mother's love is deep and powerful and I believe any woman who chooses to become a mother should understand this. I must further clarify. I speak about a mother because of the content of this chapter. But I am acutely aware that bringing a child into the world and/or caring for a child that has been brought into the world by another person covers a wide spectrum of individuals. Specifically, my words of guidance are all inclusive of caregivers who represent themselves as homosexual, heterosexual, transgender or are foster/adoptive parents. The point is that a caregiver must acknowledge the power s/he has over a vulnerable child. To that extent, words spoken to a child must be chosen with wisdom, kindness, compassion, and considerable thought so your child becomes their best self. A caregiver's words become the inner voice of the child and remain with her or him into adulthood. Having that power over a child is monumental and must always be remembered. The caregiver is akin to a superhero in the eyes of a child and can do no wrong therefore, the caregiver's words may be regarded as gospel. Frederick Douglass, famous abolitionist and author, aptly states, "It is easier to build strong children then to repair broken men."

In the best of situations, the bonding of a caregiver with the child begins in the womb. Much research has occurred between the time I was born and current times about the importance associated with bonding and attachment of a child to the primary care-giver even as early as pregnancy. A caregiver's energy and demeanor in carrying the child in her womb as well as the surrounding environmental energy establishes an atmosphere for the infant to enter. The caregiver wants to be especially vigilant to not bring on traumatic experiences during pregnancy, although not all trauma is avoidable. In the past, childbirth was more or less a medical procedure and fathers tended to not be included. The baby was whisked away shortly after s/he emerged into the world to have all of its vital statistics measured or marked. Certainly, a total reversal of birthing practices has occurred to include caregivers, which has resulted in caregivers sharing the responsibilities of child-rearing in a more wholesome and nurturing manner. Babies are brought into the world in a more soft and calm approach lessening the harshness of past practices. The baby is immediately placed on the mother's body enabling skin to skin attachment. Much work has been done on the science of epigenetics and intergenerational child-rearing practices which espouses that children are raised as the parents had been raised. We now know that those practices were not always the best, and instead caregivers are encouraged to be equally involved in ensuring that children are raised in healthy, loving, and supportive environments. Also, allowing children to become who they are meant to be without constrictions, but with appropriate boundaries, may prevent rebelliousness or at least dangerous rebelliousness.

Some thoughts about having babies and the importance of caregiving in a modern-day society:

- Life should be led with intention
- Parenting should revolve around nurturing that life into adulthood
- Together caregivers need deep self-reflection and to be deliberate in making intentional decisions about how their child/children will be raised

- Caregivers who were raised in a dysfunctional home or have experienced trauma are highly encouraged to seek counseling or therapy
- Books, articles, podcasts, and coaching are helpful tools to assist care-givers

As a society we have evolved in terms of recognizing the masculine and feminine traits inherent in all individuals. We need to recognize the complexity of the manifestation of those traits and understand that they are not generally dispersed based upon our gender alone. Ideally, men and women should have a balance-working toward being emotionally strong and productive and equally loving, sensitive, caring and nurturing. Ultimately, the job for a caregiver/s is to provide all those life skills a child needs to survive in a complicated world and then launch them, set them free to be and become their best self. Letting go of your children can be problematic for an adult who has an inexplicable need to keep their children close, and resorts to guilt and manipulation to fulfill this need. These adults need to understand why they have this compulsion and could benefit from counseling to assist in finding ways to fill the emptiness, like finding hobbies, making time to be with friends, and learning other self-love methods. There is no hesitation in asserting that raising a child or children is extraordinarily difficult under the best of circumstances. When individuals carry serious unresolved issues that interfere with their ability to manage the responsibilities of providing for and nurturing of children then help is warranted. Adults who find themselves unable to function productively must seek help to do some self-exploration and self-reflection which is an entire issue of its own, not meant to be resolved within the context of my book.

Chapter 4 -
"The Men"

We all have lessons to learn. The things that are so difficult for us are only lessons we have chosen for ourselves. If things are easy for us, then they are not lessons but are things we already know.

Louise Hay

Relationships with the men in my life have been a bit of a disaster. I am currently not involved in a long-term relationship, but would be happy to have one. That does not mean that I am willing or focused on spending lots of energy and time to make it happen, which may be a problem. It is difficult because my life is full and gratifying and frankly I have given it a shot on a number of occasions. If we think about the development of life-long partner relationships, no manual exists to guide us through the process. There are no classes in school that teach us how to find and nurture companionship. Our primary teacher is what we observe in our homes, what messages we are given verbally and non-verbally, and the guidance we receive from our parents and those family members that love us and that we trust and turn to throughout life. The home is the base from where all knowledge about our future relationships originates. It is a complicated and confusing truth. It is an evolution that happens while the family lives, interacts, and progresses through day to day living. The parents each bring their upbringings into the dynamic, most likely never having discussed the intricacies of their lives with one another and their goals of how they will raise their new family as they begin to bring children into the world. And the children respond and react from their individual genetic compositions driven by their unique biological needs and their self-centered internal hopes and desires. It is a wonder that positive, fulfilling, and committed relationships can even occur under these obscure and turbulent conditions. But for many they do.

My first male relationship was with my father. To fully understand our relationship, I must describe the dynamic between he and my mother. I was born with an acute sensitivity to just about anything and I so longed for love, especially as I got older and wanted my own meaningful relationship with a partner. Being physically close to my father always felt uncomfortable because there was always a weird sexual energy about him. I resisted any hugs, cuddling or horsing around with him and I never remember having any in depth conversations with him as a child or an adult. For that matter, I never remember speaking with any family members about life, my goals, or subjects of any significance. I did have a strong bond with my dad around football. It was more than just watching television. He and I watched NFL games every Sunday and Monday and my dad took the time to explain the game with all of the nuances of the various plays and strategies, penalties, and all other football statistics. During those times, I did feel close to him because it was our own personal routine and I loved being connected to him. Besides our mutual love of football, my father shared his lust for fun with my siblings and me while visiting family and during other celebratory occasions. He was also vigilant about attending my events with my mother. Children learn about love and companionship by how they see their parents communicate with each other, which includes discussions about plans, topics of interest, regular small talk, and arguing and the resolution of arguments. I never saw or heard any of these types of conversations where you would think living in the same house their words would have carried. Mostly, it was quiet. My father and my mother did not appear united as a force, collaborating on any number of family decisions. My mother rarely voiced her opinions or suggestions to my father.

I learned more about my father after his death than I learned during his life. He hardly spoke with us about his past, so I grew up with little information. As a result of not knowing how he actually felt about his childhood or young adult life, it is hard to piece together with a clear vision the effects of his life on me. What I can say is I wanted a close relationship with my father who was the main male role model in our home. I can say I rarely heard conversations between he and my mother about their lives when and how they met or their "dating" time so I could laugh with my siblings or tell stories about them. There was an absence of the close connections that one likes to think abounds within a family. On the other hand, when I had my son, although there were problems between my husband and me, I ensured that he had a sense of the importance of family ties with lots of affection and love, especially from me. Where my family members lacked in the display of affection, they at least demonstrated interest and gave attention to my son. In contrast, I feel my child home life was a series of scenes that were sometimes funny, many times silent. Overall, I wished to not only be seen by my parents, but I wanted to understand their hearts and souls. The distance I had from my father and my mother left me unprepared to develop and maintain a loving and lasting relationship with a man that I would have liked to consider a mutual counterpart. I learned years later after my father's passing about the dysfunctional and abusive environment within which he was raised. That would certainly have accounted for his reluctance to speak about his past. He had been especially close to one of his brothers and distanced from his other brother who had grown into an abusive father to his children. Additionally, I learned about his sister with whom he had been estranged, and who had also committed suicide. I do not know when or why, and I suppose those details were irrelevant during the time I was a child, but they must have had an impact on my father which became a factor of the environment in which I was raised. I think because of my deep sensitivity and longing for more, a part of me grew up fractured, not knowing this as a young child from an intellectual point of view. It's complex, because I knew as a child I wanted more. But I had to become an adult and do some therapeutic work to rationalize how my surroundings had actually impacted me. Because my mother had her issues about being dealt a bad card for being the middle child and her resentments about her birth order, that furthered my confusion. In fact, she was one of four children-three daughters and one brother. My mother was the middle daughter so technically she was not a "true middle child." Being the middle child however, was her perception so that was her truth. Perhaps, both of my parents shut their emotions off to survive the life they were living together and chose to ignore any sadness they may have felt. I cannot be sure because we never talked about anything. The memories that I am recalling are things I am surmising now as a middle-aged woman reflecting back on my past. It is an attempt to fit puzzle pieces of my memories together, in order to continue the self-examination work, that I am choosing to do for myself. I have chosen happiness and a positive outlook on life and hope to have those feelings prevail on my son and those around me. The process is anxiety provoking to speak honestly about my own personal perceptions of my childhood and young adult life without sounding as if I am blaming my parents for things that may have gone wrong in my adult life. But the fact is I am not blaming. All individuals are affected by the environments in which they were raised. There are no guarantees about the nature of what members of the same household can endure. My siblings may have completely different perceptions of how they saw things and to what extent they were affected or not. That neither validates or invalidates my feelings. I know I carried my longing for lasting romantic love into my adulthood and have until this point not found it.

    I met my first serious boyfriend (later became my husband) during my senior year in high school and had an intense love relationship with him, as teenagers can have. He was friends with my cousin and we all worked out at the same gym. She casually introduced us and eventually we started to "date." Basically, we spent all of our time together. From the start, we both were headed on different pathways, although I found him exciting and attractive. He was a "bad boy." I was a serious student who was enrolled in challenging classes, a number of Advanced Placement Courses, and had a plan to attend college upon graduation. I worked hard to achieve good grades and attained a decent rank in class status. I also participated in a Dance Class where I received credit for physical fitness and where I learned to choreograph dances and nurture my love for dance. My boyfriend was an average student who did not have the same aspirations as I had for attending college, but certainly had the motivation to eventually make money using his creative construction skills.

Following high school, I attended the University of Rhode Island for a year and a half studying Child and Family Studies, a Counseling Program. There I tried out for a Dance Team which I did not make. I was devastated at not being selected for the team and my self-esteem was deflated for a short period of time. I realized much later that my performance style did not mesh with the style for what the team was looking and that I was not a failure as a dancer. Still, no one offered me any consolation or even understood the defeat I had felt. Once more in my life, I felt invisible and not understood, not even by the man I was seemingly in love with. I persevered and I really enjoyed attending the University of Rhode Island, the program in which I was enrolled, and felt it was an area in which I could find success. My boyfriend worked in construction and was successful in this field. At this time our young relationship was developing and we enjoyed each other, going out to special dinners from time to time. At the same time, he had a good friend whose father lived in California. They both went to visit him and found they absolutely loved the area and wanted to move there. He wanted me to join him, but I felt he should check it out before I made the commitment to move. Eventually, upon his strong urging and my willingness to take a risk, I decided to take the chance at moving to the west coast to try it out and left school. The move proved to be quite fortuitous and fortunate for me in honing my skills and determining my future goals. California was a backdrop of beautiful scenery and had the promise of new experiences filled with hope and excitement. It was not long before I attended a class taught by Karen Voight, the fitness guru in West Hollywood who was operating a lucrative studio attended by many famous and affluent clientele. After the class, I introduced myself and we had a conversation. I expressed my interest in her work hoping to break in to her company to become a trainer. Much of the exercise programs during this time period incorporated choreographed moves and I saw an in as a viable participant in a growing industry. She was quite pleasant as we chatted and I left the class with great optimism. It wasn't long until my bubble was burst. At the next class which I attended, I was completely ignored. She behaved as if she had never seen or held a conversation with me. My discouragement was not to last, because days later I received a phone call from Karen Voight inviting me to audition for a position. This took me by surprise since I had experienced such a dichotomous exchange that being first one of amiability and the other being a complete dismissal of my existence. I was not going to let this opportunity pass by and therefore prepared for a standout audition. When I am up against proving my ability or preparing for a performance, I am all in. It may sound cliché-ish, but I give it my all, a lesson I did learn from my father. I never give up and put all of my heart and soul into my preparation. This was a pivotal juncture in my life because I felt Karen recognized in me a talent I was a little unsure that I had. I prepared my audition with expert precision, executed it, and was hired. I ended up becoming a substitute for another well-known exercise guru, Tracy York and began living the future fitness fortune dream. My days were consumed with the Studio, working the front desk when I was not teaching or taking classes. I was surrounded by a dedicated and devoted clientele who were affluent and/or famous. In this situation I had the advantage of developing all sorts of skills associated with a burgeoning industry and I knew I had the energy, the skills, and the ambition to grow with it. There I was, a young twenty-year old woman who made an ordinary decision to take an exercise class. However, in fact, my decision to take the leap and connect with a professional I had known about in an industry in which I was interested made a huge impact on my life. At that time, I did not understand how significant that choice was. It was years later that I understood.

Unfortunately, the opposite was happening for my boyfriend. He was at a standstill and not progressing while I was working long hours thoroughly loving my work in the physical fitness world. He was working and spending the rest of his free time drinking, which led to his cheating on me. I should have acted on this red flag, perhaps a prediction for future behavior. I did not. He did not support my passion or interest or even see the success that was before me. Instead, he betrayed me and I so wanted my romantic dream to be fulfilled that I appeased him. I blamed myself for his decision to cheat on me. I was engulfed in my work and he felt neglected. Instead of him speaking about his feelings of neglect, he chose to cheat. I absolutely should not have taken the blame for his choice. My boyfriend wanted to return back to the east coast and resume his work there. This was the period of time (1987) that physical fitness had become a prestigious movement. The medical field touted the benefits of how participation in a consistent exercise regimen would enhance positive health practices for those of all ages, which I could see as the growing of a whole new and exciting industry. I was at a crossroads, wanting to commit to my relationship and at the same time commit to my career. I felt I would never get this chance again, to be surrounded by this group of professionals highly regarded in the physical fitness world. Reluctantly and against the advice of the mentors around me who believed I was at the pinnacle of a truly solid career, I decided to follow my boyfriend's desires and place my career goals aside. I was hurt by his affair but I loved him and wanted to stay with him. We had spoken about marriage and like a tumbleweed, I rolled along to this next expected phase in life. I told no one about his behavior and I have since thought, that had I confided in a friend, perhaps I may have followed a different direction. It is impossible to go back to the past and change it, but it is possible to reflect on the past to garner an understanding of how the mind works to better understand ourselves for the future. I believe I left with him because I wanted to do what I had perceived to be the "right thing" and believed that he would fill that longing for an affectionate, supportive partner. In fact, I felt guilty to not follow him. Luckily, I have learned that it is not healthy to make decisions based upon guilt. It can be such a destructive emotion. After moving back, we did get married on April 1, 1989. In my rolling with the punches attitude, I allowed my mother to make all of the arrangements and although the best part of my life, which was having my son (born August 28, 1991) emerged from this union, there were all sorts of signs that we would not last as a couple. My father had his misgivings about my future husband, because he rarely participated in family events and in a nutshell we had completely different interests. I had no way of bouncing my feelings and thoughts off of anyone, especially my parents, about the important aspects of a marriage I should consider non-negotiable.

My husband was and is a good father and we shared happy times but whatever had drawn us together as a couple slowly deteriorated over time. When our baby was born, I was already starting to get frustrated with my husband. When I brought the baby home from the hospital, within twenty- four hours my husband was out drinking with his friends. And then, he went into work mode wanting to make sure that this child had everything he needed. His dedication to providing more than enough financial support cannot be ignored. I certainly respect and appreciate this quality in him, although we were both into our own unique career paths, living separate lives which became our norm. Yet, we were like a home team for our son loving and caring for him in our own ways. I cuddled and smothered my baby and young child with affection. Although I would not describe my husband (at the time) as being an overly affectionate person, he was affectionate toward our son. He was also present for the most part and shared in his interests especially when he was old enough to play hockey. Mostly, though I created and retained traditions. At Christmas I did all the organizing, the shopping, and wrapping. My son and I would decorate the tree. Dividing the tasks between parents is not unusual, but I would have loved to have collaborated and shared in the joy of working together as a family around these special occasions or holidays.

My husband did not support the zealousness I had for exploring my creativity and the time-consuming work with the teens that I had chosen to pursue with the creation of the *Off the Curb Dance* Troupe (a hip-hop performance dance group that I elaborate on later in the book). He lived his world apart from mine, which involved working long hours and then going out to drink. I could not rely on him for emotional support, companionship, or understanding. We had loved one another in our younger years and we were the first among our friends to be married and have a child. The difficulty was we grew apart and I think neither one of us knew how to repair this or that we even had the willingness to do so. I was in the midst of a highly successful venture bringing teens together to perform for a number of different audiences, in a number of different venues, and around the country and overseas. A documentary had been made about my work with *Off the Curb* by Susan-Cobey-Williamson who had been a student at New York University. She had seen us perform in New York and was impressed. She followed me for three years as she created the documentary. She captured the energy, the intensity, the creativity, and the overall purpose of *Off the Curb* and wanted to honor the worthiness of such a Dance Troupe. The completed documentary was shown in a few film festivals and did well and eventually was aired on the Public Broadcasting Channel. I'm sure my husband admired my talent in his own way, but he did not appreciate the significance of the work or the acclaim given to me by highly reputable authorities in the industry. A lot of people thought I was a single parent because he was never around. He did not understand the fulfillment I gained from my work with *Off the Curb* and the relationships I shared with the kids. However, he could be quite generous with the teens and often treated them to snacks or gave them money as a token of validation of their work, as a relative might treat a niece or nephew. His gestures were kind. With my professional aspirations, he chose to distance himself from the entire experience, which was hurtful and an indicator that he just did not understand something about me that was deeply ingrained in my soul, while many others did. I wanted a partner that would connect with my essence and I with his. Perhaps, because of the environment that I had come from, I accepted our remoteness as normal for as long as I could, clinging to the idea that things could change.

When I lost my father, I lost a piece of myself and entered a very dark place. The grief I experienced as well as the grief that consumed my family was overwhelming. Grieving the death of a loved one is complicated and deeply upsetting to say the least. The person experiencing the myriad of emotions needs compassion and time to absorb the finality, the sadness, and the anger. It is a long-involved process and I needed understanding from my husband more than ever. That was not to happen. Rather, he resented my withdrawal and actually made a stabbing statement to me. He said, "I guess I have to kill myself to get your attention." I chose to stay away from anything or anyone that did not bring me happiness and unfortunately my husband fell into that category. Our lot was sealed after those words and we divorced in 2001. I knew it was a difficult time for our son as divorce is for children, but I will say my husband and I committed to keeping the ramifications of the separation as amiable between us as possible to ensure that our son understood he remained our top priority. We had joint custody and continued to share the responsibilities and joys of parenting. Unfortunately, the very good friend with whom my ex-husband had traveled to California committed suicide and through his tragic loss, I believe my ex-husband came to understand the enormous sadness and the horrific emotional trek I had gone through. To our credit we have since found a way to become friends and we were always dedicated and loving parents to our son.

The break up with my husband was difficult especially because of the pain I felt my son had to endure as he learned to adjust to living in two different spaces. As far as my feelings were concerned, I think I had left the marriage emotionally long before our official divorce and to some extent I breathed a sigh of relief. I needed a pause after the divorce and frankly was not ready to enter into yet another committed relationship. Meanwhile, I dated a bit and out of the blue after closing the *Off the Curb* studio I was contacted by my teenage crush. He wooed me and took me on an amorous escapade which I completely bought into because of my incessant desire and belief in that ultimate romantic love. He showered me with gifts and loving attention. The hopeless romantic part of me felt like I was living out the movie *The Notebook*. But my story did not end with that unrealistic everything tied up in a neat bow ending. He left me with virtually no explanation after a seven-week interlude. I was hurt and devastated thinking that maybe I had not found my forever mate, but at least I had temporarily found someone with whom I thought I could enjoy and get to reconnect. Someone I thought was having a good time with me, as I was having with him. But that was not the case. He had been in the process of divorcing his wife and I filled some narcissistic fantasy for him. And I was taken by his charm because of the longing for love that he filled in my heart, even if it was not sincere. I sort of gave up thinking and believing that I was ever going to find that one person with whom I could build a life and just proceeded on with my gratifying work and raising my wonderful son. But inside, I knew something was missing. I had spent a number of years with my first boyfriend who became my husband and then my ex-husband and with trepidation opened myself up to the opportunity for love when this man approached me. I would not say I was desperate to have a man, just longing for the right person to uncover the deep yearning for a connection. I realize love takes time to blossom, but it has to start somewhere. And this self-centered man, rather than connecting, took advantage of my vulnerability and I allowed it.

Shortly after, a couple of events happened in my life. I made the decision to finish my work with *Off the Curb* and my son was about to graduate from high school. I was faced with the dilemma of what I was going to do next professionally and truly entered into a transitional state of emotions if such a state exists. I had all sorts of painful emotions but it was time to let go of my successful dance troupe as well as close my studio. With my son graduating and leaving for college, as every parent can relate, a barrage of emotions smacks you in the face while watching your child leave the nest. This is when I met a man who is against everything I believe in. I cannot fully explain how I allowed myself to participate in such an unhealthy situation except to say that the hopeless romantic in me once again emerged its unrelenting tentacles. Inside, I was a jumble of anticipation, fear, some sadness, confusion and no clear direction.

Given my state of mind, I was vulnerable and found myself stimulated by the thought of seeing this intriguing man.

I was lost in my aloneness. And so, this man became a welcome distraction as I figured out what my next career steps would be. I knew this was a bad decision because he was already in a relationship. I rationalized in my head that we could be friends and that maybe he was not serious with the other woman and their relationship would not last. So, I agreed to meet up for walks and they were pleasant enough. About two to three months into the "connection" we did become sexual and that added an intimate component to our non-relationship. It was odd and dysfunctional and I knew this. It was not a relationship because he did not have the capacity to be involved in one. It was a connection. Everything about it was wrong for me. It was one of my lows in life and I knowingly went forward and agreed to involve myself with a philanderer who lied, cheated, and had no reasonable aspirations to live a healthy and productive life. I found him physically attractive and realized that however our sporadic meetings could be defined the end result was not joyful. In the end, if I was going to be involved in a relationship, what I truly wanted was a man who was consistent and reciprocated the generosity that should exist between two individuals who care about each other. He could never be a long-term partner because he was deeply narcissistic and had too much unresolved trauma. Also, I could not handle his elusiveness and ambiguity.

I had the notion that I was the special one and that was why he continued to return to me. I created this idea because of my longing to have that one special person. In fact, he fed my fragmented self, the broken part of me. If I look back to my childhood when I was alone all the time, feeling solo, I realized that this man reinforced that feeling in me. Even when I sat with him, I felt alone. In my higher self when I felt good and everything was going well I did not need his presence in my life. I didn't look for it. But during those times that I felt down in my lower self he was who I would go to. I longed for him to be the type of a good and loving companion that he just was not, and even though he showed glimpses of those positive qualities from time to time he was not the person I wanted him to be. He had that ability to charm me and others but truly it was manipulative behavior that drew women in. His personality flaws and my hopeful, romantic heart kept me clenched in and I fell for his dishonesty and insincerity. This dynamic was completely unhealthy and it was almost like a self-fulfilling prophesy perpetuating my fragmented self instead of accentuating my healed self.

Knowing that he could not participate in my world did not mean that I was going to leave his world which, in a word was chaotic. As he shared with me his past background including his childhood and family issues, I certainly was empathetic, and intellectually understood why he could not be a stable and true partner to me. But knowing something intellectually and having feelings do not always align. Of all the men in the world, and with all of my education and motivation to do well for others and the world, there is no logical explanation as to why I would have become involved with this person. I thought I could change him because of how he led me to believe that with his openness, he was bringing me closer to his inner soul. In reality, he reinforced my core belief of remaining alone because it required very little effort on my part to maintain this non-relationship. It was better to have someone who was hollow and dishonest than to be without anyone. I have worked so hard to execute the projects and practices that I believe in. I have been trained and educated and believe I have been a force within a wonderful community. And so, I too as others, have made some unhealthy choices which have caused me pain and confusion. My human side is revealed through this incongruous behavior. My hope that he would become the solid, compassionate, and kind man belongs to me. It is not possible for him to be this idolized person that I had created.

After proceeding with my life and fulfilling the goals I established-going to school, getting my degree in holistic counseling, establishing my workout studio, developing creative projects and now entering into private counseling, I would like to enter into my own new power. I realized that I cannot blame him for my attachment to him. Instead I need to release his hold, wish him well, and move myself into a higher vibration of goodness. I need to open myself up to the possibility of a person who can enhance my qualities and not place myself in a situation where I am forced to make judgements about the character of a person with whom I have chosen to associate. This required lots of work on my part, but in the end, I believe it was the only way that I could become my best self and reach my best potential. It was not his fault for holding me back. I held on to him perhaps to keep me in my safe zone. I allowed him to prolong my inability to move forward. That part is over.

The Take-Away:

I have realized that all the men in my life have the same thing in common. They were not there for me one hundred percent. They did not support me and they did not see me. I would say my father fell into a slightly different category, in that he did see me as his child, but had his own issues clouding his judgement. He had his skeletons living inside of him, but he wanted us to be loved and showed us in his own individual way the best he could. I have also realized that I have a pattern of choosing men with personalities and behaviors which are the opposite of what I teach, how I live my life, and those qualities I long for. It is an important flaw for me to share because unless we are willing to be honest with ourselves and face our darkness, then it is impossible to heal. I want to motivate people to live their best lives but even a teacher sometimes fails. We know what is best for us but we do not always make the right choices. I feel as if I had to retrain my mindset to alter the neuropathways to think in a healthier manner and not romanticize a relationship that did not exist, once I became willing to do the healing work. I learned much by reflecting on what drew me toward the men I chose and I am now spending my energy manifesting the man with whom I would love to develop a relationship.

Another take-away is when you have a father that you love deeply but you do not have that affection piece, it is hard and confusing for a young girl. Your dad is the first man you love and you want him to protect and keep you safe. My father as I have described, had that "uncomfortable" energy but he was the one who was funny, happy, loved birthdays, celebrations, and made each one of his children feel special, under his own conditions. There is no other way to explain, except to say that the dichotomy of his personality was perplexing. A young daughter really does not have the skills to analyze the subconscious mind as it develops, while simultaneously undergoing the maturation process of changing in every biological manner possible. What I witnessed in my father's and mother's relationship I certainly did not realize as a child. However, looking back in hindsight, I see that my mother was so connected to her mother that her marriage was somewhat compromised. I knew my parents loved each other but because of my mother's connection to her mother, she was often absent from her husband. Interestingly, my father was absent from his parents and married someone who was not one hundred percent there. As a sensitive child, I believe I internalized the idea that you do not get the "whole package" which unfortunately becomes a core belief. My husband had great qualities but he was unable to fully love me unconditionally. I didn't have anyone instill principles about the types of healthy attributes to look for in a partner and how important it is to associate with whole men to share a relationship. We never had those deep conversations. I followed my heart and took chances. Fast forward, I attracted wounded men. My attraction to these men makes sense to me because my father had a missing piece, married my mother who had a missing piece, so the theme of my life was there is a missing piece in all men. As a result, a part of myself was empty and I closed myself off to allowing people in because they would not understand me anyways. Thankfully, I was able to develop an internal creative life. I am slowly starting to understand these aspects of my personality so the people with the missing pieces are no longer the individuals to whom I am attracted. It is not easy to find people who are evolved, have done their personal work, and are the healthiest version of themselves.

Guidance:

In the take-away section, I explained my point of view from my own experiences as a heterosexual woman. When I think about the ideas I have to offer as guidance, I want to be clear about how influential our caretakers are to each individual as we develop and mature into our adult beings. The term "primary caretaker" is all encompassing, inclusive of all LGBT individuals and various configurations of family structures. The environment that is created in the home including the interactions between couples, or in single family situations or others involved in the raising of a child or children, influence and impact that person's future ability to develop their own relationships. Specifically, our partner choices are what we learned as children from our caretakers. What did the caretaker model as far as healthy relationships and what did the individual internalize? What decisions did the individual make intrinsically that are playing a role in his or her life now? The answers to those questions are found by taking a look at yourself and evaluating the relationships with those that you are currently involved or have been involved. Are you picking a healthy person? Are you picking a person that has all the qualities that you like and for which you long? Who you decide, hopefully, as your permanent partner should be a whole person knowing that the process getting there may not be entirely smooth sailing. A child's relationship with their primary caretaker tends to set the tone for future relationships. If those relationships are loving, healthy, and open than most likely the outcome for the future is positive although there are always exceptions. I would caution an individual to conduct a thorough self-reflection on their relationship to their first caretaker to become aware of possible red flags or energies that do not quite fit into that person's comfort level. In my particular experience, among other things, I never observed my parents argue and so it took me many years and much work to understand the importance of how to appropriately deal with anger. Naturally, anger is a normal emotion, usually disguising pain and it needs its proper attention to release it in a healthy manner. Also, some of my learned behavior had to do with not using my voice to speak my truth, which resulted in a variety of issues related to the suppression of my feelings. I had to learn how to gain my confidence to be able to assert myself as well as to employ self-care practices like deep breathing to release tension from my body. These are the red flags that we want to address and find some assistance in uncovering so that we do not carry the behaviors associated with them into our adult lives. If we don't heal the broken pieces of ourselves we are going to keep attracting people who are broken.

When we have had trauma, betrayal, or disappointments especially as children, there is a piece of us that gets hidden away, buried, or protected. That is called the fragmented self and Eckhart Tolle (spiritual teacher and author) refers to it as a "a pain body that is floating inside of us." For me I spoke about the solo-soul. I protected it, took care of it, and did not let anyone have it. An abuse victim may place their fragmented self, deep within and there is a hole of emptiness that they continually try to fill their entire lives. Someone else with a fragmented self may hurt so badly that they push everyone away and never allow anyone near them. Sadly, a young child or an adult who has experienced a major life trauma event could become a fragmented person and may be so wounded that they cannot be healed.

Individuals suffering in pain protect themselves in different ways, depending on who they are and how deep the fragmented self is. If the hurt or the broken part of the individual is not brought to the light or the surface, it just becomes more magnified. We all have a broken piece of ourselves on some level. Key to becoming the best version of ourselves is to admit, acknowledge, and begin to do some work around this broken piece with some deep self- reflection.

In developing healthy partnerships, it is important to go slow, taking your time to get to know the person. There is nothing wrong with being enchanted by the newness and excitement of the relationship and actually enjoying this phase. However, it is critical to remain based in reality and not ignore the red flags that emerge. This is especially true if you have had a history of unhealthy relationships. Throughout my life and into my early marriage years, I neglected to speak my truth and I simply went about my life the way I had been guided in my childhood. We were raised to do what we were told, be polite, and to not rock the boat. The structure was so ingrained within that even when I began my path toward healing and spirituality, the unhealed portion of my spirit dragged me down, allowing the dysfunctional self to take control. We want to work toward becoming aware of the power of dysfunction and to begin the soul-searching process so that piece of you is not unconsciously making decisions for you. Instead, you learn how to have control over the dysfunction and can decide what is best for you. Counseling, therapy, or coaching will offer an individual a means to explore the past, the painful feelings, the negative functional patterns, and guide you through methods and skills to turn the dysfunction around in a safe environment. Reading inspirational or healing books is also productive.

Chapter 5 -
"Mother- Son Bond"

> By giving children lots of affection, you can help fill
> them with love and acceptance of themselves.
> Then that's what they will have to give away.
>
> Wayne Dyer

There is one part of my life where I am wholeheartedly full of gratitude and joy. That part is with my relationship with my son. When he came into my world, I was complete. I needed nothing more and my soul and every inch of me was filled with pure love. My work with *Off the Curb* and my other creative ventures satisfied a deep need within my soul, but never in the way that my son's birth brought me ultimate fulfillment. He will always be that one person no matter what, that will forever fill me with eternal love. I simply cannot imagine a world without him. I knew that I wanted to have a child and felt that surge of emotion when a woman knows it feels like the right time. To be absolutely transparent I also knew the moment I conceived. From the minute I knew he was living in my belly to when he was born on August 28, 1991, my heart melted and I was instantly in love. He had dimples in his cheeks and I will always remember the instant that nine-pound, six-ounce miracle bundle of joy entered the world. My precious boy was an expressive child and I was attuned to his every move and sound. I sensed all of his wants and needs as a baby and then later as a toddler and young child when he started to speak. When he was to have his first shots, the look he gave me is imprinted in my memory forever. He was apprehensive and so was I. I knew I was not going to be able to protect my precious son from the pain he was about to feel, as well as the inevitable pains that would come along as he moved through his life. It was a frightening reality that I had to confront upfront. The impossibility of sheltering my child from the future obstacles he would have to face. I wanted him to only know joy and peace, which of course was unrealistic. At the appointment, the doctor poked him and my son glared at me with inquisitive eyes asking, "How could you let me feel this pain?" Every instinct in my body was to protect him and I was there to immediately comfort him as he interacted with a stranger who hurt him. I realized there was no way I could have ever let my baby be unnecessarily hurt without hovering about him consoling him with all of my energy.

My mother-in-law (as well as his father) had also fallen in love with him, not in the same way as me, but none the less she wanted to be a preeminent person in his life. She had struggled for years with excessive alcohol consumption and I shuddered a bit in allowing her in, but made it clear that I so welcomed her, if she could stop drinking. From that moment forward, Nana never had a drop of alcohol again and became an extremely powerful force in my son's life. We were fortunate to have her live with us, and the bond that developed between the two of them exists to this day. When I was younger, I vowed to myself that I would never have a household that resembled the one created by my mother and my grandmother. However, the living arrangements turned out to be entirely different and my mother-in-law, never interfered in our lives. She retired to her own room at the end of the day and allowed us the privacy to be a family. I came to really appreciate her presence since the nature of my work with *Off the Curb* required so much time. I did not want to drag my son with me to all of the rehearsals and traveling events when it was not necessary or convenient for his life. As a matter of fact, he perceived his Nana as being the only one who was there for him, a thought he shared with me as a young adult in a conversation we were having while visiting with each other. That was a painful statement to hear, and honestly almost brought me to tears. But I knew he had the right to his own perspective and that for parents it is at times difficult to hear how your child perceives a given situation. I knew and still know that he loves me, and understand that this special relationship with his Nana was a comfort and support to him during his childhood. She was and is a warm- hearted woman with whom everyone felt at home. There is just both deep joy and deep pain in being a mom and the learning continues always. I knew when I became a mother that I wanted to create a warm, loving, and supportive environment for my son, where he could grow, develop, and thrive. My son had a free-spirit as a child and was always on the go exploring the novelties in his world, playing his games with enthusiasm and energy whether imaginative or with toys. I recall one specific time out of many when he was thoroughly enjoying his time at Legoland where he received a "driving license" after driving one of the little vehicles and was just so thrilled. All of the sweet, innocent pleasures that brought him pleasure brought me happiness and I wanted him with me all the time. At a young age, as I began my work with *Off the Curb* and my studio classes, my son did join me on many occasions. As he became older before he reached his satiation point being with his mom, as most kids will do, he attended performances and rehearsals with me. He had the fortunate opportunity to be around a variety of people that spanned the scope of personality, sexual orientation, and race. He was exposed to a world that celebrated inclusion and diversity. Those encounters helped to develop his ability to communicate, to understand compassion, and to be able to successfully maneuver within a myriad of environments and situations. He is an open-minded, kind, and understanding adult male. Those are the qualities I attempted, sometimes knowingly and other times not so knowingly, to impart within him. He has lots of family and friends who loved and continue to love him. I consider my son to be a twin-soul because I feel when he feels. Certainly, my feelings are not the same as his, but I can confidently assert that my intuitions about the physical or emotional pain he has during crucial moments are accurate. He knows he can turn to me for advice, comfort, or assistance when needed and that I will actively listen and not judge. And although I share my concerns or fears about some of the decisions he makes, our relationship is open and our ability to communicate is direct and honest. He also knows I am there to congratulate him on the many accomplishments he has achieved and continues to have.

    I'm sure it was not always easy for him growing up. When my father passed away, it was extraordinarily difficult to explain to my seven-year old son what had happened, and for him to absorb the finality of death at such a young age. On the day my father passed, my husband and I knew we needed to be prepared to tell our son the truth once he came home from school. With some assistance from a counselor we told him, "Pop hurt himself so badly he died." With that, our son burst into tears, a sadness that no parents want to see in their child's eyes or hear in their voice. He understood death and that his grandfather was gone and not coming back. He had lost a puppy. However, he also knew that this loss was very different. The days that followed were a blur for me and I was functioning as a robot helping with the arrangements and with my mother. The children in the family were given the option to attend the wake, the funeral, or both. My son opted for both and was truly a stalwart young man throughout the process, describing my father's body as cold after viewing him and tolerating all of the protocols involved with funeral rituals. There had been an exorbitant amount of media coverage because of my father's status and the circumstances. He was also able to read and with newspapers around, he saw the tragic details and asked me, "He shot himself?" I answered him with a "Yes, he did." I was numb and doing the best I could. At that moment, only my son's well-being mattered and was the primary concern. I really did not know what effect my father's passing would have on him. I only know I had to be there to comfort him, in spite of my chaotic state of mind. We did speak later on about my father's suicide as he matured and understood, to the capacity that anyone can understand about someone's suicide. It is a devastating act that each person must reconcile on his/her own, I think by talking and processing. We do continue the conversation as milestones occur, such as the day my father passed or his birthday and only when and if appropriate.

Three years later, after my father's death, my son had to deal with his parents getting a divorce and all of the emotions that accompany that disruption to his young life. He was ten years old, and as a child had no concept about what had happened between his father and mother that brought them to the point of breaking up. His perception through the eyes of a ten-year old was upsetting because he saw me leave and did not comprehend that I was not leaving him. When he was a young adult and understood more and as I had mentioned previously how he had shared the importance of his Nana in his life, I felt it was important that I explain my reasons about why the marriage had to end. I shared the complicated dynamic of his father's and my relationship as best I could through my eyes and why we had agreed to joint custody. I'm not sure at the time that he grasped why he did not live with me permanently. Therefore, I thought I needed to explain why I felt he should share his life half the time with his dad when he had better capacity to understand. After our conversation, the divorce made better sense to him or at least he honored my feelings and somehow, I think our relationship shifted after I explained my feelings and decisions. I also realized that although the divorce had been difficult, my son always had the love and attention from both parents. I also felt grateful (when I could separate out my own feelings) that my son felt so strongly that he had had his Nana very intricately involved in his life, traveling with us when necessary for the performances of *Off the Curb* and giving him lots of security and of course more love.

I must admit I did become the ultimate helicopter mom after my father's suicide, scared that my son would hold his feelings in and not express them to me. I knew that this was my issue I was projecting onto my son, and knew that I needed to resolve the fact that he was not my father and that I had raised him to have strong coping skills. We gave him unconditional love. Most parents cannot bear the thought of any tragedy broaching on their child and that of course was and is me. I do have confidence in his strength, intelligence, and his good common sense. Still, as his mother I can never cease to worry about his well- being while at the same time only hoping that he finds happiness and fulfillment in his life. I want him to always be free to pursue his dreams and aspirations and include me in his world under his own conditions. I believe I raised my son as an honorable man who will make a wonderful partner to a lucky woman and will bring his positive qualities in creating his own family. He is kind, generous, my most ardent cheerleader for the work that I do, proud of my projects and respectful of all of my hard work. Luckily for me, my son has learned the balance of merging family with his individual needs. Family is important to him but so is his independence. He brings me happiness, pride, and peace.

The Take-Away:

When I became a mother, I had no idea of how deeply I could feel for another human being. It is unlike any other love I had ever experienced. From the moment my son was in my belly, I could feel his presence, which only increased as I began to feel those magical twitches of life moving within me. When he entered the world, I held him and I immediately knew and embraced my job to protect him always from any danger or uncertainty. This role was such a huge, scary responsibility that I can only say the fear of this daunting new position was equal to the depth of my love for my child. Nothing in life was ever the same, having my heart and mind always on the presence of my child. On every level I felt deeply. During his childhood, when my son and I were together he had one hundred percent of my attention. I truly saw him for who he was and continue to do so as an adult. I was enamored by him from eating his little bagels to his roller blading at four years old and his dancing to Michael Jackson songs. I just wanted to watch him grow and loved marking the milestones that children reach during their developments. As a baby, a toddler, and a young child I held him for as long as I could, probably too long. I carried him around with me knowing how fragile this time of holding him in my arms was. He would outgrow this stage and this time would eventually change. I tried to be attentive to him, attempting to understand what he was thinking and feeling. I exposed him to different activities and encouraged him to try different hobbies. Some he liked, others not so much. I just had to accept that. Some things were the things I wanted for him and not the things he wanted for himself. I must say I had to develop the insight to know, that he knew what was best for him even at a young age. Sometimes, like many parents think, I wonder if I was too involved in his life and pushed him away. I don't think this was the case because as an adult, my son remains very close to me. We both enjoy each other's company as well as have productive and meaningful conversations with one another. He is comfortable bouncing ideas off of me and I respect his thoughts and ideas.

I believe as a divorced mother that I lost a little bit of my son's childhood and missed out on some things. He lived in two homes so segments of his time were lived without me which was really hard. In fact, it was very painful and I had not prepared my mind for this major shift in parenting. I left our home in Saunderstown because my work was in Newport and my husband and I agreed to joint custody. My son was fortunate to have had his Nana stay with him at his dad's house and she was extremely helpful and supportive to all of us. When I did have him with me, I was determined to make our time quality time. I tried to impart my teachings and guidance onto him as much as I could, while being careful to listen to all that he had to share and to interact with him as much as was physically and emotionally possible. I always strived to be a positive influence in his life since he was only with me for half of the week. To our credit, my husband and I were both committed to the well-being of our son and did not allow our issues to become his.

Each child has his/her own unique outlook on life and I have always made myself be aware of who my son was and how he chose to operate in the world. From earlier times as a young child until present as an adult, my son has solid ideas and knows the measured steps he needs to take in order to attain his next goals and dreams.

He has taught me and what I have learned is that I have done everything I could to instill values and discipline in him. I have to trust that I did a good enough job that he will take those values I instilled in him out into the world and live by them, even when I am not around. For many years, as he became an adult I had an intense energy around him. Even though I was not with him I still had a grip on him energetically, and I had to learn how to loosen that grip and let him learn to trust in his own energy. I needed to use a mindful energetic release to self-talk myself into trusting him, the universe, and the angels to always protect him, to take care of him, and to guide him to make good decisions. It is my prayer and mantra every single day of my life. I send him angels and good energy. and protection and lessons so he has the ability to make those important choices. Each parent has their own way to adjust to the separation process that occurs between parent and child over the course of their lives, and this is my method. Our relationship is such that he does share his ideas with me and asks my opinions on things. In turn, he is one of my advisors and helps me sort through my ideas. He is very rational and helps me see the logical side of the various things I present to him. He has always been my cheerleader and has given me books and cards that reiterate the message to follow one's dreams. We reciprocate those sentiments to one another other. I think I have done a good job in raising him to be independent and not co-dependent. Guilt does not work on him. He is not a person to be manipulated to get him to do what you want. I will ask him a given request and he will either say yes or no. And I think this is very healthy and a great quality. He is not cruel or selfish, if he is unable to honor a given request or task. He is direct and honest, knowing his ability and boundaries.

Guidance:

This chapter encompasses so much having to do with the love between mother and son but it cannot avoid discussing parenting methods and skills. Yet, it is impossible to offer comprehensive guidance in the artful, emotional, sensitive, and complicated parenting sphere

because being a parent is so personal and dependent on each individual's past experiences. So, I will speak from my experiences and from the lessons that have seared through my soul. My main topic is about mother to son bond, but I also must emphasize the importance of understanding the bonds between parent and child in an all-inclusive society that encompasses all configurations of gender relationships. In all situations the common thread is love, in whatever capacity it is given and received.

Partners must make a conscious decision to model a healthy relationship with appropriate boundaries and a common, unified vision of their hopes for their family. If the partnership becomes unhappy and a divorce or a separation happens, then certain components need to be understood and addressed. There is always going to be a sadness that goes along with the divorce or separation because the dissolution of the family in its original state is extremely altered. Not having your child with you all the time was one of the most painful lessons I learned in my life. There is no getting around the dilemma associated with the impossible decision of reconciling one's personal unhappy feelings in the marriage and the hurt that follows for the child/children. When parents choose to end the relationship because of the unhappiness between them, the hope is to model for the child/children the healthy practice of choosing happiness. Usually there is one parent who leaves the home. Again, the hope is that the parent who leaves will model appropriate behavior demonstrating the ability to care for him or herself in a healthy manner. That parent should make productive decisions from a place of strength while assuming the change in life-style, as opposed to falling apart and operating from a weak place making unproductive choices. The reality, however, is waking up on some days in a new home alone, knowing that the child/children is with the other parent can bring on a surge of overwhelming sadness and loneliness. It is not unusual to second guess the decision to divorce and to question whether it was better off to simply have remained in an unhappy relationship in order to be with your child/children.

The deciding factor rests upon the established environment in which a child/children is raised. The child/children will always sense tension between the parents if it exists. Therefore, it is best for the child/children to be surrounded by love and to witness observe healthy relationships and eliminating exposure to unhealthy relationships. When a marriage or partnership ends, an adjustment period of learning how to be alone is an inevitable and painful reality. The parents are doing the best they can to meet their spiritual and soulful individual needs, and will miss out on some of their child/children's lives. But they are ensuring and demonstrating how important it is to feed that part of yourself, which in turn is a lesson for the child/children. If it is possible and a couple is contemplating breaking up, then the couple has to know that divorce has a major impact on a child/children and prepare for the unrest that will follow. The adults are going through a major change in their lives, but so too are the child/children. Divorce is second to death in stressful loss.

The child/children must be given the voice needed to process through the feelings. The best the parents can do throughout this change is to help the child/children understand that all people go through difficult life changes. And it is paramount that the adults behave with compassion and strength to teach the child/children resiliency so they can understand that not everything is within their control and the challenge is to learn how to manage the difficult times. Parents must work together in the interest of the child/children to provide emotional stability. And as amicable as it can be, the divorce will leave a mark on a child/children. That mark needs to be processed by the child/children as they move into adulthood and begin their own relationships. They will find it necessary to understand the effect divorce has had on them based upon their individual circumstances.

The relationship between a mother and her son is special and significant. The bond is not easily described. It is not romantic, it is not a friendship. Explained concisely, it is a mutual caring and deep unconditional love. A son looks to the mother for what a woman should be like. But it must be noted, that current society is rapidly changing to include homosexual marriages and families. In consideration, what remains most important in care-giving of a child is the love between the child and the parent. It is optimal that for both sons and daughters that they have role models who demonstrate what has been previously referred to as masculine and feminine traits. Those lines are blurring somewhat and it behooves our society to become mindful about their choice of words as we move into new and progressive realms, seeking not to exclude individuals when discussing parenting. We want our children to be kind, loving, resilient, caring and healthy beings, so as parents our task is to help children develop those traits to the best of our ability. As a society, we should also realize that not all children are entering into the world having grown up in a family structure with both a mother and a father. Our institutions therefore, should recognize the diversities in family structures and especially in our educational environments move away from the "mommy-daddy" model. The language rewording has to reflect the diversity of the current family dynamic. And finally, parents need to look at themselves for an honest reflection of their parenting strengths and weaknesses. As parents we have to be honest about who we are. Some things we are good at and with other things we struggle. It is critical to own up to our faults.

Other thoughts to consider. For a variety of other different reasons besides divorce, some parents find themselves raising their child/children as a single parent, having to fulfill both the masculine and feminine roles. An astute parent will welcome other family members or friends to assist in the care of the child/children which will enhance the love given and received. If the home is healthy and the adults surrounding the child/children are well-rounded and positive, then everyone benefits. Some children arrive with the assistance of a donor which has helped a number of women carry their child in their womb and experience pregnancy and childbirth. Other children may have had the opportunity to be adopted or cared for by a foster parent. In this case, some parents will share with their child where they came from in a natural way when they determine it is appropriate for them to understand. There is always a chance that the child will want to know their biological parent. Although challenging, it is encouraged that parents tell the truth, be open, and allow the child to pursue what s/he needs to do. If the parents have created an intense bond, then meeting their biological parent is not going to change the relationship. The two parents that raised the child have to be confident in their role and see their child/children for who they are. In all cases- donor, adoption, fostering and the addition of a step-parent- whoever enters the fold, it is the love for the child/children that matters. The more love the better that person becomes. A new person will not replace the parents that raised the child/children. That person may offer yet another perspective and viewpoint about the complex world in which we all must navigate. Parenting requires such an assortment of emotions and responsibilities with a true commitment to selflessness, that when a person enters into it they must be prepared always to expect the unexpected. It is the most fulfilling role a person can choose to take on or not, with a constant flow of joy and doubt.

Part Two

Dancer

Chapter 6 -
"*Off the Curb*: Its Inception"

Dancers come and go in the twinkling of an eye but the dance lives on. On many an occasion when I am dancing, I have felt touched by something sacred. In those moments, I felt my spirit soar and become one with everything that exists.

Michael Jackson

Along with giving birth to my son, I also gave birth to the *Off the Curb Dance Troupe*. My dreams had been temporarily on hold when I left California, but as fate would have it, I decided to combine my love for dance and my skills in teaching physical fitness. I opened the Jackie Henderson Fitness and Dance- Home of *Off the Curb* Studio. And in all matters of creating and birthing, I molded (like a young child) this amazing group. It has been dissolved for a number of years but lovingly lives forever in my mind with the ups and downs of its existence. I gathered a bunch of rambunctious, diverse, and sometimes troubled teenage girls and boys who wanted to dance and trained them to become a dynamic performance troupe. They were required to refrain from drug and alcohol use and commit to weekly rehearsals, learn and execute the rules of the stage, while expressing through their body, a love for dance, specifically hip-hop. As a young, white woman during the sporadic volatile times of the 90s racism, this was no easy task. Hip-hop is much more than a music form applied to rhyming rap lyrics and is better described as a cultural movement. After its onset in the late 70s, hip-hop exploded into a cultural revolution during the late 80s into the 90s and continues in its vibrancy today. Its origins began in the South Bronx section of New York City and has become increasingly popular with its commercialization into mainstream culture within the past years. The historical roots can be traced back to African oral traditions as the "voice of an otherwise underrepresented group." Much has been written about the exploitation of black Americans as hip-hop "has pushed out of urban areas and into the suburbs. Hip-hop has had a tremendous influence on mainstream fashion, television, movies, advertising, and language." I loved the dance form from its onset and was passionate in sharing it with audiences.

I needed to recruit students who were seriously interested in dancing amid the various distractions that most adolescents experience on a daily basis. Most teenagers have a natural inclination to party and in that atmosphere to dance, but few want to devote their personal time to participating as part of a team which entails responsibilities and obligations to the members and to its purpose of entertaining others. With much persistence, a dedicated group formed and we enjoyed countless performances. We were enthusiastically received by a variety of audiences of all ages as a creative and productive performance group. Some may have not understood or appreciated the music, culture, and lyrics associated with hip-hop. But the presence, the energy, the talent, and the sheer professionalism of the performances were extraordinary and impressive, by the variety of students who were members of the troupe. *Off the Curb* became a well-known entity of the Newport culture. The city of Newport, Rhode Island is world renowned for its historic architecture and its rich cultural art, along with the many historical events and activities that have occurred on this island city. Newport for the most part was an ideal venue for a troupe such as the *Off the Curb*. After all, both the Newport Jazz and Folk Festivals have been, and continue to be, attended by people from all over the world who admire the many famous musicians who have used Newport as a place to introduce new material. These festivals have assisted in easing the way for cutting-edge musicians to enter into a somewhat conservative atmosphere, following in the footsteps of the classic artists who preceded them. There has always been and probably always will be a tension between the undercurrent of those artists who seek to disrupt the status quo and those who remain well within the confines of the old guard who fear any sort of change. I consider myself a proponent for those who want to take risks as well as those who want to explore new creative options. I am always ensconced in my love for dance and especially the pure, organic movements associated with the rhythmic beats of hip-hop.

To not acknowledge the connection of hip-hop to young black Americans is an injustice of the artform. Interestingly, in my role I experienced being judged for my race, a white woman participating in a hip-hop world, although the Dance Troupe was a diverse group of teens. Many kids of all races from the surrounding communities found a connection and a love for all things hip-hop. Many sought out the chance to be part of the *Off the Curb* dance classes and to become part of the troupe. Maybe, hip-hop began with rebellious young black teens, but rebellious other teens were drawn to it as well, relishing in the soulfulness, that may have not been appreciated by their parents. When the dancers pointed me out as their choreographer and director, it was obvious that many audience members were surprised to see a white woman at the helm. On one specific occasion, I was approached by a local black community leader who wanted to meet with me and I did not know why. I did agree to a meeting. When we met the woman asked to pray with me, an odd request that I succumbed to seeing no reason to decline. She then proceeded to let me know how disappointed she was about my being a white woman in charge of the *Off the Curb* Troupe. She felt hip-hop was a genre grown out of the black American culture and should be taught and spearheaded by Black American leaders.

These encounters were strange to me and left me somewhat annoyed. I had conceived the idea of reaching out to teenagers to share a passion and a skill that I believed would benefit them while having fun. I was never thinking of this in racial terms. I was doing what I was doing because I loved to dance and to inspire the kids with whom I worked. It was never my intention to offend anyone's race or culture. I had worked strenuously to bring this idea to fruition. I certainly can acknowledge all of the racist behaviors present in day to day life for most Black Americans, and would not diminish the unfairness and absolute horror of discrimination. I sought to create an all-inclusive environment around the universal art of dance. I felt somewhat disheartened, but carried on. I profoundly believed and continue to believe in the importance of inclusion of all individuals and support all efforts to do away with the terrible biases that continue to exist in our current society. These beliefs were conveyed to all who participated in *Off the Curb* as well as all the projects that I continue to create and direct today. There is no room for those who want to exclude. In addition to the hard work of practicing and preparing for performances, much time was devoted to conversations with the young people. I knew I had to be open, honest, compassionate yet firm with the adolescents with whom I worked in order to create a positive and productive team. We became like a family and I cared for them dearly and as a result a magical bond united our spirits toward a common goal. These young people brought many issues to the forefront, underlying traumas, neglect problems and internal conflicts that erupted from time to time during the school day. In addition to being the sole Choreographer, Director, Producer, and Manager of my Dance Troupe and Studio, I also was a "counselor" and confidante to my dancers. One of my dancers had become involved in an altercation and misrepresented my program to the point that the school administration was threatening to have her expelled. I basically forced my way into her world to help her formulate a plan to advocate for herself. I spoke with her about the altercation and once I felt comfortable that she felt sincere remorse, I assisted her in resolving the problem. I needed her to know that in spite of her poor choices, I still cared and that she had a person who believed in her goodness and was willing to support her through this crisis. Remorse and forgiveness are always possible if someone is willing to do the reflection and the work to get there. In the end, the administration accepted an apology and she suffered the consequences of a suspension with no expulsion. She graduated with her class, meeting all of the necessary academic requirements.

For me, *Off the Curb* was so much more than a fabulous dance troupe. I became a wiser, stronger, and better person through my experience of working with the many pre-teens, teens, and young adults with whom I interacted. These young people were with me as I raised my child, as I lost my father, and as I divorced my husband. We valued our tight bond and we used dance to express and decompress through synchronized and high-powered movements that came from the heart.

The Take-Away:

The take-away for the inception of my work with *Off the Curb* begins with the messages my soul was giving me and the "unable to ignore" guidance from the universe. I knew a few things about myself that were intractable. I had to use my creativity. I had a gift for dance and choreography and I had a charisma about me. I say this not to brag and not to toot my horn, but as a reality about who I was at the time and who I have continued to be, although I am more mature and seasoned. When I returned to Newport after my adventure in California, I was approached by a fellow teacher to assist in teaching classes which were beginning to evolve as jazz funk and she knew my skills. My workout classes were intricately choreographed and I was a dancer, although I had taken a hiatus from dance. I did end up working with her, but it wasn't long before I began to feel constricted and wanted to teach in my own space doing those classes I wanted to develop. I am grateful that I took that path without hesitation and with confidence. There is nothing wrong with doing the work you love in the manner in which you choose to do it. I also know I have the ability to draw individuals in and to motivate them and with teenagers it can be quite a challenge. But, I have always respected teenagers and children as people with individual interests, strengths, and weaknesses, with their own thoughts and ideas. I knew that when I began to work closely with young people, that I could learn from them as much as they could learn from me. So, what transpired was a melding of the just right ingredients for a spectacular sojourn into a space I loved with people who could trust my vision and move it forward with their own sassiness and talents. I had always loved hip-hop as a teenager and embraced it as it became more and more popular. I was drawn to the music and immersed myself in this culture that fed my soul, put it on fire, was colorful, and brought me joy.

I loved watching the teens use their natural ability to dance while knowing all of the music. When I would teach them the steps and moves, the choreography looked better on them than it did on me because they had the street look, feel and attitude. I would give them the dance and the choreography and they would take it to a whole other level. This collaboration of talents so inspired me to want to share my art and creativity, to break through into something that had never been done. And we did it and I never gave up. I am proud to say that I instilled values and purpose into the groups of dancers with whom I worked. They saw that they could travel and get out of Newport and off the island. They learned professionalism and how to carry themselves and speak politely to our hosts. They also learned how to deal with difficult and unappreciative individuals, thankfully, not often. Once, I was asked to leave with my dancers and to not complete a performance because the Principal of the school felt one of the dance gestures was inappropriate. The dancers touched their chests under their shirts with their hands imitating the beating of a heart. It was such an innocent gesture, and unfortunate that an adult could be so ignorant that he found this dance move inappropriate. This experience allowed me the opportunity to process the interaction with the troupe in an honest and compassionate manner. I let them know they had done nothing wrong.

During those fruitful years of orchestrating this creative endeavor, I knew the work was important. I was changing lives and giving the kids a platform that built confidence and expanded their outlook on life. The combination of both the creative and the interactive aspects of this troupe built character and developed life skills. Reflecting back, I see how important the work was. In hindsight, not only was I offering all of those outlets, opportunities, and expertise for the kids, I was also creating inclusion, diversity, and acceptance. I was crossing racial, gender, and sexual orientation barriers in the early 90s and throughout the years. *Off the Curb* instilled these necessary beliefs into the culture thirty years ago. It was very natural for me to be accepting. I felt it was essential to let the kids be who they were and to provide support while they explored their individual attributes, personalities, and essences. I am grateful that I had that capacity without realizing that I was helping normalize something that was not so normal. When I think back, I have come to understand how my work and time with *Off the Curb*, was at great cost despite giving me lots of self-satisfaction and my own personal development with sheer enjoyment. I was lucky to have had my mother-in-law helping me with the care of my son, providing the option for him to travel with us or stay at home. Many times, I had to make choices and sacrifices in order to follow my dreams and passions. Ideally, I would have appreciated my partner supporting my vision and work. In life, when partners are not in agreement about career paths, a person has to decide what is more important- your relationship or your dream. In my situation I did not consciously made a choice, I just stayed focused on my work. I was living my passion and fulfilling my dream.

Guidance:

This guidance section is more of a dissertation about how I see the world as part of who my essence is, my passions, and how I answered those passions. It is about what I experienced with my work and how I want to convey my deep feelings and beliefs to the reader that in my opinion are necessary in making the world a better place for all of us. In the discussion about my words of wisdom that I would like to share with you, the reader, I feel a need to speak about hip-hop and its origins a bit more because, there is a direct correlation to that and the teens with whom I worked. Also, hip-hop for some and certainly with its birth represented a misunderstood artform that generated a whole lot of negative generalizations. Again, not for all, but for some. And this speaks to the greater issue of society's affinity to generate stereotypes and mistruths of that which is unknown. Hip-hop was born during the disco era. In the urban parts of our country and in the Bronx, New York specifically, young adults did not relate to disco and needed an outlet, a means to express themselves, their love, their hate, and their frustrations and to have some fun. The elements of hip-hop were created. They consisted of Mc-ing (rapping), B-boying (dancing), DJing (turntabling), and Graffiti (artform). There are volumes of material explaining the details of each component but suffice it to say hip-hop began and exists as a creative force that came out of nowhere. There is no doubt that currently hip-hop is an ingrained artform world-wide and for the most part though it may not be enjoyed by all, it is certainly appreciated for both the entertainment value and its commercialization.

Hip-hop represented what Americans do. It was a rebellion of sorts, similar in impact as the protest music that was born against the Viet Nam War and the norms of the time, which prevailed among American youth during the 60's and 70's. Young adults created hip-hop propelled by their need to be seen and heard, and to protest against their poor living environments and the conditions that sustained their oppressive lives. As its popularity grew, so too did the business end. Russell Simmons, chairmen of Rush Communications, along with Rick Rubin (Producer) co-founded the hip-hop music label Def Jam Recordings and created the fashion lines of Phat farm, Argyleculture, and Tantris. The explosion of hip-hop took on a life of its own as beat makers such as Run DMC became well-known and other artists such as Beastie Boys, L Cool J, Will Smith, and Jazzy Jeff, went on tour. Many more artists joined in the frenzy and millions of followers became avid fans and hip-hop was secured in mainstream culture. The rap lyrics began as fun party starters. As the raps progressed, they often mirrored the anger and territorial issues associated with various neighborhoods of both the east and the west coasts and were likely incomprehensible to white middle class culture. For the young adults who used their artistic expression through rhyming and music, this venue and genre empowered them. To not acknowledge that a society of gang life existed for some, is to not fully understand the intensity of the hip-hop culture. And by no means am I advocating the gang life. I know it's there and I know it's the life some young adults choose as a way to fit in or have a pseudo family, or to be part of a group or to make money. I would like to believe that as a society we could get to the core of why certain individuals get drawn there and how to help them find and envision other alternatives. But I also need to acknowledge the rawness of their emotions which is often transmitted through hip-hop music and culture. I think it is fair to say that some of the artists who became famous reflected their lives authentically through hip-hop. It is their truth.

It is important to remember that it is not an us and them although a race barrier is present. At the same time, we have to remember everyone is a human being struggling and even though someone looks different than you and has a different lifestyle than you, that lifestyle might look scary or something you do not want to be involved in, those individuals are still human beings.

And I know that saying, "I think it is human nature for people to be drawn to like people," can be interpreted as a controversial statement to some. I would like to clarify. Young people like to hang out with young people. If you see people from your native country, you are going to speak your native language. Black people tend to be drawn to black people. White people tend to be drawn to white people. Like is drawn to like. Older people to other older people. Dancers to dancers. Athletes to athletes. But an athlete must respect a dancer. A white person has to respect a black person and a black person has to respect a white person. We all have our own belief systems and should be able to share ideas. If we can get to the point that we know and share our own values and let others share theirs without there having to be a winner, without someone being right and someone being wrong, what an achievement that would be. Why can't people enjoy and respect other cultures and beliefs? If you are strong enough and confident enough in your own belief system then you should be amenable to others. In the same vein, it has always baffled me that some religions profess and directly teach the doctrines of their religion to elevate their belief system and to downgrade those who do not follow them. They extol the virtues of their believers to be the "chosen" ones who will be rewarded and saved while the rest of the world of individuals will be lost somehow. As a society of compassionate and intelligent human beings we have to be flexible. A flexible mind is a healthy mind. You have to be able to accept someone for who they are and in turn expect that acceptance to be reciprocated. Integration is honoring differences and appreciating likenesses. If you do not have that, then we are always going to be at war with other people, other religions, and other races. Let people live their lives.

Chapter 7 -
"Off the Curb – Passion for Dance"

Nothing is as important as passion.
No matter what you want to do with your life,
be passionate.

Jon Bon Jovi

We are each born with our talents and sometimes it takes time to understand which ones will surface and resonate. I was born a dancer. The love of dance is in my bones, my heart, my mind, and my soul. It is interesting to trace the history for my love of dance from my childhood until today because it is such an integral part of who I am and continue to be. As a young child I took ballet lessons but quickly learned that that was not going to be my forte'. I actually hated it and ended up quitting those lessons. Instead, I gravitated toward jazz and funkier movements as opposed to the more classical and precision steps of ballet, taking classes in my middle school years. I perceived this genre as "cooler" and more in tune with my natural rhythms. Then, the movie *Flashdance* was released and Michael Jackson released his album and music video "Thriller." He performed the "moonwalk" during my high school years and I became entranced.

    I participated in the Dance Program at my high school as an adjunct for physical education credit and I joyfully hopped on board, not that I was uninterested in athletics. Dance class meant I could dance every day and it just fed everything about me. It filled a huge hole in me, that gap for the persistent longing for more. What was important about my participation in this program was that I began to forge a passion that would only intensify as the years progressed. Often times, individuals are uncertain about the path that life will take them on and do not fully understand the hints, messages, and signs that the universe provides. But those abstract ethereal sparks are stored within the memory until they are eventually ignited. And I stored plenty in those years, not conscious that I was doing so. I did however, catch the bug for performing. My dance teacher's classes were designed around dance routines predominately using show tunes like "A Chorus Line," and "Cats." She also brought guest teachers in such as Adrienne Hawkins, a well-known choreographer based in Boston, who taught us how to take up space on stage. As a good high school educator, my dance teacher encouraged us to use our creativity and she supported our autonomy with our own unique creative expressions. I loved performing on stage and the thrill of having huge audiences.

    At our first show at my high school, we had eight hundred people in the audience which filled it to capacity. I remember I was performing a trio with two other girls and we opened up the second half of the show with me in the middle position. When the curtain opened, all you could see was me and the whole audience started cheering. I loved the power of being center stage and the internal energy of feeling liked and admired. It propelled me to perform with even more vigor and with the intention of pleasing the crowd. Standing before a cheering crowd is an extraordinary rush of positive vibrations that just makes you want more and more, I suppose like a "rock star." I loved everything about dancing- the moves, the music, the costumes, the rehearsals, and the performances. I truly did not know then that this love would simply keep growing until I finally made it a huge portion of my life's work. Dancing made me and continues to make me happy. It made me feel connected to myself and others. I wanted to emulate the performers in *Flashdance* and dance for the love of dancing. During this time period at sixteen, I began choreographing hip-hop and brought break dancers into some of the routines. My dance teacher always provided us with challenging and interesting material but she loved it when we took the initiative to experiment on our own. Naturally, I took the challenge and I believe gained my confidence in the ability to use dance as a creative and soulful outlet. When I went off to college, I wanted to pursue my studies in psychology but I also wanted to maintain my passion for dance. When I didn't make the dance team, my confidence was deflated. I didn't know the difference between a modern dance company and what I was doing. I thought the reason I didn't make it was because in high school I was a big fish in a small pond and then I went to college and I wasn't as good as I thought I was. This rejection killed my spirit. Reflecting back, I realized that I had no one supporting my efforts, no one to explain the harsh reality associated with competition in the dance world. I had no conception of the artist's goal of fulfilling his or her vision and therefore initiating the difficult decision to cut dancers who did not fit the vision. Rather, I stopped dancing for five years. I had never really considered becoming a professional dancer. I was never surrounded by any local role-models who had pursued and attained this occupation.

When I left Rhode Island and moved to California I was afforded more education, not in a school but with my interactions with those in the business of physical fitness who merged exercise with dance. In California, I observed individuals having awesome careers and they opened up my eyes to opportunities I felt could be within my reach. One of the classes being taught was called Cardio Funk which was very popular. I did not participate in it because of my hiatus from dance and my broken spirit about my "failure." Yet, it registered in my mind as something that appeared energetic, high-powered, and fun and I knew I would come back to it at some point in my life. In California, the building blocks to enter this space were literally at your fingertips, unlike the east coast where the expansiveness of physical fitness and dance had yet to take hold. However, upon my return back to the east I had decided to dance again having been approached to teach something akin to cardio funk which had begun to catch on in a limited basis throughout the country. I realized that I was a good dancer. I suppose I had to come to this realization by going through what I had considered a failure but was really a detour. I had to hustle to find fitness and dance on a professional level in the northeast. My pursuit, my struggles, and my continued spirit to never give up stems from that inner drive, to fill the holes of wanting and knowing there was more to life. I carved out my niche based upon my passion and drive. I traveled to Boston for classes eventually trying out for the Reebok performance team. They were in the process of creating a hip-hop team and out of a hundred people trying out for this team I was the only one they picked. They didn't know where to put me because they didn't pick anyone else and so they put me on the Reebok performance team. (It was a fitness team which was foreign to me but fun.) My dancing was calling me back. I started creating ties with Reebok and other well-known fitness leaders in the Boston community. At the same time, I started to go to New York to take dance classes where I met more dance and fitness professionals.

All of these experiences were preparing me for what was going to become my professional life for the next sixteen years. I had decided to start a hip-hop dance troupe of teenagers because I was inspired and believed it would be fun. I thought "I'll just get some kids and do a performance." I asked a friend who worked in the community with groups of teens, if he knew of any young people who would want to dance. He found two young girls who were interested. I taught them a routine and then the three of us did the routine together in downtown Newport. When I think back to this time, it does boggle my mind a bit because I was not impeded by any doubt or constraints. I had an inherent belief, "if you build it they will come" like in the movie *Field of Dreams*. We were dancing for fun and I knew other teens would have fun dancing as well. Too often, we allow ourselves to stop the impulses that may have lasting positive results. Those spurs of the moment performances did just that and with a spark of ingenuity, the stored messages were ignited. The sequence of events was as follows. I started teaching hip- hop dance classes and taking these two girls out for shows and then more kids started seeing them and then they wanted to join in. During that time, hip-hop was not an option taught in a dance studio. I was the first one in my area to teach hip-hop in a studio. I don't know about the whole northeast, but I was the first one who put hip-hop in a dance studio in Newport, RI. It was street dancing before that. It was street battling. I was actually organizing and choreographing it, bringing it to the "masses" and I am proud that I acted on my instincts, my impulses, and listened to the sounds of the universe. I encourage you all to try it. We would put on shows in the street, and with our boom box just start dancing. The lesson is: if you want to write well, you must write every day, if you want to run a marathon, you must run every day, if you want to perform, you must practice at a performance level every day. The kids were like magnets attracting each other from Newport, Middletown, and Portsmouth. Initially, I danced with them and we performed shows anywhere that would allow us to perform. The Newport Yachting Center was in its beginning stages of hosting festivals and I saw that as a great venue to be seen and without my realizing, those shows became an excellent marketing strategy. We were never paid, but these performances gave the kids multiple opportunities to dance and to spread the message about *Off the Curb*.

I didn't know much about the dance world. I thought because I was twenty-five that my chance to be a professional dancer had passed. My career was done. But little did I know that the prime age for dancers was twenty-five to thirty- five. I learned that years later. The creation of the dance troupe was not about me because I thought I was too old to be a dancer with the kids. My goal for *Off the Curb* was to develop these kids into great people, great dancers, and to see how far into the world I could take this program. I always put them on the stage and sat back and watched my work. That was very fulfilling for me. I didn't feel like I was missing anything. I didn't feel like "God I wish I was out there." I was happy I wasn't out there. They were doing such a great job. I just loved watching them and the audience's response to them.

I cannot complete my sequence of events without mentioning a person who supported my work. I called him *Off the Curb's* benefactor. He loved to dance and was the kindest, most caring person ever. He took an interest in what I was doing and shared the passion. Along the way of creating and building a viable business, there are those individuals who believe and support the entrepreneur's endeavors, understand the vision, and the goal. And I had those people who helped me in various ways including providing storage and office space which may sound inconsequential but is not. Every building block and kind gesture in a work in progress helps to contribute to the whole. It is like parts of a machine have to all be in working condition to have the machine fully operate. This was how I was able to institute my studio, which included both dance and physical fitness. I needed to have my own space so that I could implement the programs and classes that I chose without interference from other administrators or managers who had their perspectives. In addition to my studio work, I reached out to the local Middle school and taught after school classes. I was able to do this with the help of a grant issued by a Task Force that wanted to offer students productive activities as opposed to having them hanging out on the streets. Some of those after school students found their way to the studio and began to participate in the *Off the Curb* dance classes and some auditioned for the troupe.

Where did the name *Off the* Curb originate? As I researched what I would name my program, I came across a quote in a magazine, "His moves came from straight off the curb." I was like "Off the Curb, hmmm." Since the Task Force had given me a grant, I needed it to be community based and justify the reason this program should be funded. It was an obvious segue to promote my concept as a no drugs, no violence program- a program where kids had to behave in positive ways. The dance moves came from the streets and we were getting the kids off the curb. Finally, I needed a logo and came up with the *Off the Curb* guy who is posed with his legs forward, wearing baggy pants and wearing a "peace" sign necklace. With the completion of the concept, the recruitment of kids, my vision, and my dance expertise, I felt my entrepreneurial spirit overcome me with joy and satisfaction. I had found my vocation.

To my credit and to the kids with whom I worked, the troupe began to improve by congealing as a team and perfecting their performance skills. I continued to travel to New York for classes and this placed me in the epi-center of the latest and greatest of the trends happening with the hip-hop and dance worlds. I networked with professionals and one in particular. I did not hesitate to inquire about the possibility of bringing my troupe to perform at a fitness conference that she had told me about. She allowed us to perform and shortly after, *Off the Curb* was invited by others. We experienced a domino effect that made the troupe well- known. At this point, we still were not being paid but we were all enjoying the thrill of travel and performing. Eventually, as we became better known, I was able to charge for the performances and began writing more grants. The dance classes were requested in large demand and I had some of the students begin teaching. We performed locally at school assemblies, at New York City fitness conferences, in Harlem at the annual Special Olympics Event, in Washington, DC, and many other events. The dancers in the *Off the Curb* Dance Troupe had extraordinary experiences traveling and performing. They enjoyed the rudimentary conditions of piling in a van, driving for hours, and squeezing in hotel rooms for the sheer delight of dancing. They had the opportunity to visit cities and see other performance troupes one of whom was called "Culture Shock." They were adult hip-hop dancers and left a lasting impression on both myself and the dancers. We all learned much from watching their dance moves that transformed us for the better, toward hip-hop as opposed to funk.

I could see the positive effects the troupe had on the kids as well as the positive effects on the kids who participated in the dance classes. I wanted to keep these feelings going for the kids probably at some detriment to my own personal life and marriage. But I was committed and as opportunities presented themselves, my inclination was to grab them. I found a conference that was being held in Portugal and I applied for it. They accepted us and wanted us to perform. We needed to raise $10,000 to cover our traveling expenses and I have no idea looking back on how I did this, but I did, including bringing my son and mother-in-law. The Portugal trip was phenomenal and life-altering because of the learning the kids gained about the different cultural practices among countries and the humane similarities among individuals. I was assisted by the *Off the Curb* benefactor, who was able to facilitate a Master Class that I taught. The Master Class was with all the rival dance groups, crews who all battled each other. They were from different parts of Lisbon and they were not friends and instead were quite competitive with each other. Out of the blue, an American choreographer arrives to give a master class and all the rival dance groups showed up and my dancers performed. The Portugal people's style was funk and not street. So, when they saw *Off the Curb* perform, they were blown away. I taught the class with about a hundred students who all got along and had fun. It was such a moment in history for us all and it was beautiful. The performance at the conference went really well. For clarification, funk is more fast paced with fast music. Street is the use of hardcore hip-hop music, more hard hitting, with more of an urban feel to it, more intricate. It is important to note that choreographed dancing was not part of the original hip-hop culture. Mostly, people were free style dancing as well as free style rapping. Hip-hop dance evolved from b-boying also known as break dancing. The b-boys used to battle each other. That's how different dance groups formed, challenging who was the best. The culture was the same in Portugal, all about pride and being the best known in what you loved. The ability to have all these young people embrace each other's cultures around a positive creative outlet such as dance, music, and performance was truly a chance of a lifetime. And in spite of the fears and anxiety that my kids felt in traveling away from home and their safety zones, I am certain they were all forever changed and as their leader, I am forever grateful.

The Take-Away:

I was disappointed when I moved from California back to Rhode Island, but what I learned from my time there was that fitness could be a viable career. I knew that if I wanted to be successful that I would have to work twice as hard because there were so many more opportunities in California. I would have to go to bigger cities like Boston or New York to take classes and to feed my soul. In California, I saw a whole other world that was possible and that I could create. When I returned I enrolled in Rhode Island College to study Athletic Training and attended the program for three semesters. As part of the program, I had an internship at Providence College as a trainer to the Providence College Basketball players. At the same time, I was also going to New York City for fitness conventions. There, I was able to see Patricia Moreno teach a class called Cardio Moves. My jaw just dropped as I watched her. She was so beautiful and a great dancer who totally inspired me. I just knew intuitively that I could do this same work and I was destined to do big things with my life.

In June of 1992, the first *Off the Curb* performance debuted. It had begun with smaller performances and then I procured studio space and kids kept coming to take the classes. The troupe was taking up much of my mental space because I was in creative mode and it was difficult to concentrate on school work. I ended up leaving school because I needed to be fully committed to this endeavor to make it successful. Leaving college and starting a dance troupe was risky but I just kept following my passion even though I was not completely sure about my next steps. I can only say that when you are feeling so incredibly inspired and motivated, you have no choice but to follow your dreams. Some people lean toward security and finishing college and getting a job and making money. That was what my husband would have me do. He wanted me to become a nurse, contribute financially to the family, and provide healthcare through an established company, since he was self-employed and did not have those benefits. His preference was that I finish my degree, get a job, and do the dance work on the side. I understand his practical point of view, but that goal was his and not mine. I was not the practical one.

I was consumed and motivated to become an inspirational teacher and choreographer and put my vision into action. My interests were a passion that fed my soul and I couldn't stop those urges. I just had to keep going and develop my art. This persistent desire was a calling and when you are called you have to answer it, even if it is risky. If I failed I didn't care what people thought. Failure was not on my radar. There were times I did think, "How am I going to make money?" But I didn't have to worry about finances at that time, though my husband would have liked me to be more financially responsible. He would say things to me and I would shrug. I would not concede. I just kept going and tried to figure out ways to monetize my work, but money was not the driving force. I applied for grants and I started to charge for performances. I must say I was not very savvy about the pricing and the monetary value of the troupe's talent and our shows. It was "trial by fire." I always put my heart and soul into my craft and I know that was appreciated and respected. Many of the people who started with me have remained with me throughout the years because they continue to reap the benefits of my teaching. I have been told by other current fitness teachers that I have been an inspiration and role model for them.

I provided a positive and healthy outlet for the kids in our local community as well as for kids outside of the island. The after-school programs were grant funded and free to the teens but a nominal fee for evening drop-in classes was required. Many of those students were motivated to attend those classes so they could eventually audition for the *Off the Curb* Dance Troupe. Whether they were trying to improve skills or not those evening classes provided another outlet for those who loved to dance and wanted more time to do so.

Guidance:

I can only say that you do yourself an injustice when you do not follow your creativity and use the gifts with which you were born. Your love for the creative talent inside of you will gnaw at you continuously until you decide to do something with it. So, figure out your best plan and go after it. You cannot wait for others to tell you how to proceed, if you do not have a vision for yourself. When others attempt to give you their opinions and ideas, those thoughts will have more of a tendency to confuse you as opposed to guiding you forward. Along with relying on others to give you a map or an outline for your vision of success and its total mish-mosh of information, be cautious of naysayers. For every idea you may have, there will be a person who will offer their two cents to point out all of the pitfalls and risks. If you have the yearning passion to express your creativity and are willing to fight to implement it with eagerness and fortitude, then go for it. Once you commit, you cannot look back with doubts or you will guarantee failure. That is not to say that you will not have bumps in the road. You will. And that is not to say that you cannot turn to trustworthy friends, family, or consultants for advisement. You can. But you must drive the ship and you must be selective about the advice you choose to take. And if you fail, it will be yours alone to examine as you find the right formula for your vision and you will, if you stick it out.

I loved what I was doing and the fact that others thought I was good at it was an appreciated perk. I had an innate drive and passion for hip-hop. I was young and doing what came natural to me. The passion became contagious. Others began to follow me and joined in.

I had a talent for dance and I had a vision. Once I had those ingredients, there was virtually no person or situation that was going to stop me. I was not sure how it was all going to come together, but I knew that it would. I would recruit amazing young dancers who were going to be inspired to execute my vision, because of their love for hip-hop. These dancers felt the magnetic pull of this colorful and creative artform. It was a fire in my soul and in theirs and together we followed it. The drive was beyond our control and all I thought about was how I would surpass the energy of the last performance, which I attempted always to communicate to my dancers. It certainly was no easy task. I considered them to be intelligent and passionate people with minds of their own, but they were young and also had other interests and responsibilities. Some of the dancers grew up in difficult environments and needed a little extra attention. Those teens should have known more about basic life skills and habits but they didn't because of their upbringing. Sometimes someone has to take you by the hand and teach you. I was that person for some of my dancers. At the same time, I had the good fortune to expand their horizons by bringing them to a bigger world.

I embraced all individuals and included them in the dance troupe, if they were selected from their audition and had the desire to perform. I was always on the cusp of doing the work for the dance troupe while challenging the norms of society. Not that I was an activist. But because of my work, I was a representation of a kind of "movement" that placed me in the limelight. I believe that you have to look at someone as a human being and not as someone separate from you and different. *Off the Curb* broke through all demographics including all ethnicities and cultures. I felt that my inner thoughts and beliefs surfaced authentically to those around me that either needed to listen or happened to be there to listen. We have to realize it is important to understand that everyone is doing the best they can to raise their families and there is no reason to be separate. America's history has been complex and disturbing and we have to acknowledge this. Historically, the power was predominately in the hands of white individuals. And on top of this, we are a media driven culture that feeds us twenty-four- hour information more than just reporting but propagandizing. At the beginning of hip-hop, television shows were mostly about white families, until the brilliant Norman Lear created sitcoms featuring black families. These sentiments are not to highlight our past atrocities, but to at least acknowledge that they existed. And against this background, the emergence, growth, and ultimate explosion of hip-hop, a unique and exciting artform entered the mainstream and became a force to contend with in teenage culture. And I embraced the artform, exuded my passion, and found a tremendous amount of personal success which I have never regretted. I became and am a better version of myself, although I am not finished developing, because of my relentless desire to follow my passion.

I would highly recommend anyone who is contemplating entering an unchartered territory of creative design and implementation to:
- Read inspirational material about your passion
- Study the lives of famous people who have risen above their obstacles
- Listen to podcasts that offer meaningful guidance and advice about how to handle doubts and fears

- Research your craft, idea, skill, or methodology
- Learn how to map out strategies and realistic plans
- Be creative about procuring financial support
- Build your self-confidence by participating in activities and events that bring you joy
- Know your worth
- Never give up

Maybe the initial idea has to be modified using the creative spark that initially inspired you. That's not giving up. It is addressing reality. The idea may not be fully feasible at the time in the way you would like it, but may need some extra attention or additional materials. Perhaps completing a portion or portions until ready for full fruition is a more attainable option. You may even choose to venture into a different direction. Whatever the case may be, it will be your choice as to how the conceived idea will be completed. Know that transformation is a constant part of the process.

Chapter 8 -
"*Off the Curb*- The Power of a Mentor"

> The delicate balance of mentoring someone is not creating them in your own image, but giving them the opportunity to create themselves.
>
> Steven Spielberg

I have spoken about my belief in how the universe plays an integral part in our destinies. Given this belief, I therefore see life as having no accidents or coincidences. Situations and events happen for reasons because they are supposed to and we are supposed to be vigilant in remaining on the lookout for the lesson, especially if we want to be the best versions of ourselves. The same is true for the individuals who became members of my dance troupe and those who took my classes. I have no logical explanation about why the many teens entered my world, but I can unequivocally say that they brought much happiness and enhanced my knowledge about life. I never had one specific passionate direction to follow prior to the creation of *Off the Curb*. I just followed the inspirations that came to me. I have described myself as a person with a happy essence, although as a young child I had an emotional longing for more.

Inside lurked a creativity that thankfully filled the longing holes and I never seemed to take a conventional or expected path. When hip-hop began, I instantly fell for the sound, the beat, the culture, and all else that accompanied it. I was born a dancer and cannot imagine my life without it. The match was secured and when I had the chance I decided to enter into the hip-hop world by developing a hip-hop dance program. I mentioned prior that I recruited two young girls, with the permission from their parents of course, took a boom box and began dancing with them in downtown Newport. This was after trying college out, after returning from my adventure in California, after getting married, and after having a child. I envisioned an idea that was deeply tied to dance and I proceeded to make it a reality in the form of a program. I have realized that I am a person who does not need to wait for all the dots to connect at a precise moment for me to act upon an idea lodged within my body, soul, and mind. I am the type pf person who has to act and see where I go and then connect the dots. This is how I created *Off the Curb*. I created a dance troupe and an outreach program housed in a studio with exercise classes included all which developed from an initial spark of an idea.

Life is not a linear course to follow. Many of our institutions falsely emphasize the importance of planning your life's goals out, and checking off the boxes that bring you to the final end. I am the end result of the opposite, which does not mean I am a freewheeling fly by night whatever happens, happens person. Somewhere internally, my gut had the instincts to ensure my safety and success. I do not measure my success by how much money I had or have, although I would have loved to have been more financially secure during the *Off the Curb* years. In hindsight, I could have handled the financial end of my program better. I do measure my success by the lives I have touched and the lives that have touched me. I allowed my passion to drive me forward, living, and breathing this project. I recruited young adolescents who had an interest in dancing and encouraged them to join the classes and to have fun.

One way I recruited participants involved organizing a lively performance showcasing the first teens with whom I worked which took place at Thompson Middle School in Newport. At the end of the performance, I appeared on stage to honor my dancers, to explain my program and to invite audience members to visit an Open House at my studio. Needless to say, the audience members were completely enamored by the skills of the dancers on stage and secondly were surprised that the dancers were being led by a white woman. It was uncommon to have a hip-hop performance led by a white woman, since the hip-hop culture had originated in places occupied predominately by people of color. Many teens were curious about who I actually was as a hip-hop choreographer and wondered "How did she know how to dance?"

Many teens had lots of free time on their hands, and needed and wanted something to do besides hanging out on the streets or at home. For those reasons, they attended my Open House. Subsequently, a number of students visited my studio every day and never left after that initial visit. I cannot say it was always pleasant because as young adolescents like to do, they behaved in silly ways, often teasing and jesting about. However, the teens had respect for the dancers and me and never interfered with my teaching process. Not all of the teens chose to dance initially and were satisfied to be in the onlooker position. When it was time for the dancers to learn a choreographed piece, the onlookers watched and remained respectful, never disrupting the process. I suspect they felt too intimidated to participate. I also suspect by watching they may have played the moves over in their minds and in order to gain the confidence they felt they needed to jump in. In fact, it took one young lady a full year to decide to audition for the troupe. She had come from a family of dancers and knew she had talent, but she had had no training and was intimidated by some of the other dancers. Others remained in the background somewhat longer. Those teens were on the periphery of what was happening. I felt strongly that as long as the kids were not disruptive, that being in the studio was perfectly acceptable. My philosophy was to welcome the children into the experience whether it be performing or observing.

I taught at various schools in after-school programs besides teaching classes at my studio, and there too, I also welcomed teens who wanted to watch. Some of the teens never danced, yet enjoyed the music and the dancers. They had a sense that they belonged and were happy being a part of a group even if from the "outskirts." I always held the belief and still do that students of any age, teens or younger should be treated with respect and understanding. Adolescents are at the age where they are struggling to find out who they are and where they fit in. I mindfully created an environment where teens were safe and accepted whether in my studio or in places where I taught outside of my studio. Many teens do not have the confidence to just jump in and begin dancing if they have never been taught the moves or they simply prefer not to dance. However, they are happy to vicariously enjoy the experiences they see as well as love the music. I did not want them to be uncomfortable because they preferred not to dance. I provided an all-inclusive space for teens to enjoy a performance experience while discovering their own individual passions. I was empathetic to this process and understood that hip-hop dancing was not for everyone. But all teens want to belong to something in one way or another, without being judged. By maintaining an open and welcoming atmosphere I was able to attract a variety of teens who had the choice to become involved as little or as much as they chose. As the interest grew, I realized I was onto something that audiences wanted to attend and enjoy. I implemented more structures into my program in order to develop the professionalism of the troupe. Students were required to audition. This included learning choreography and performing it back while being evaluated for ability, skill, and an innate feel for the rhythm. I also encouraged a personal display of free-styling moves as part of the audition. Eventually, from the auditions, I created a solid and committed group.

In the spirit of inclusiveness, I had lost my job of counting the dancers in when one of the onlookers took that role on, with her measured and determined voice reiterating, "5,6,7,8." That seemingly small role of responsibility became a valuable job for an extraordinary shy and insecure person who found respect and attention from the dancers. I think it is those small acts of disseminating trust that allows for the development of relationships and a sense of belonging, as I reflect back on how I taught and functioned. I also firmly believe in second chances and in the flexibility of rules under certain circumstances. One example was when one of my potential dancers lost her chance to audition because her fear took over her. She was scared and intimidated when it was her turn to audition. She ended up loaning her sneakers to another potential dancer who had forgotten her shoes and lost out on her time slot. In tears to her mother, she recounted the story and her mother subsequently contacted me to see if her daughter could have the opportunity to audition. I allowed it and it turned out to be an excellent decision because she became one of the stars of the troupe. Too often, adults become fixated on inconsequential rules and order and do not see beyond the parameters that they have created which ends up being an exclusionary tactic, breaking the spirit of teens. Perhaps, because I experienced being a solo-soul, the not being seen, the internal isolation, I wanted to have other teens not experience that predicament and could see beyond the artificial boundaries. In turn, I think the teens appreciated my attention and compassion and therefore wanted to do their best to please me. They wanted something different in their lives and I gave them the alternative through my work with *Off the Curb*. The young people who came through my studio and outreach programs were looking for something to connect to and hip-hop dance gave them the outlet.

A word about Newport, RI where the troupe was based. Like many other small cities and towns in America, old tensions die hard. The city had and continues to have a mixture of cultures and ethnicities but also has had the unfortunate leftovers of segregation practices, which is a difficult topic to address. When some of the teens saw the performance of my dancers at Thompson Middle School one black young lady observed and commented, "I saw kids that looked like me." Although they were surprised that I was a white woman leading the dancers, they were immediately connected to the mixed-race group. The dance troupe was always a combination of black, white, brown, Asian, and all other races and ethnicities by virtue of its organic existence. I never made a concerted effort to construct the groups as a mixed conglomeration. It happened organically. My work broke the expected norm because of my motivation to have kids enjoy hip-hop and because of my desire to fulfill my creative ambitions. I wanted to take this troupe as far as was possible and these teens accompanied me throughout the adventure. I was viewed as the one token white girl in Newport doing the one thing that stereotypically "should have been done" by a black person. Typically, the north end of Newport was dominated by the black population and the southern end by the white population. And the middle of the city was somewhat of a mixture. To see me dancing hip-hop or directing a hip-hop group was extraordinarily unusual at the time (early 90s). As painful as it can be to face the truth, I point this out because it was my choice to pursue my love of hip-hop, not knowing that I was breaking a preconceived mold. It was an authentic, natural, and fun implementation of an idea that shred stereotypes and was indicative of one of my infamous risks that I chose to pursue. Speaking recently with a black woman who had been one of my teen dancers with *Off the Curb* she reflected saying, "Jackie was the Tiger Woods of dance." What a great compliment to receive. When I think about that admiration bestowed on me and the zeal with which I approached my work during those years, it bothers me that as a society we feel compelled to place one another in such tight-knit boxes of preconceived notions. I truly want to dispel the temptation to pigeonhole people. Instead I would rather shout, "See what is possible?

Dive in! Follow your passions! And do not let those pre-conceived notions become the barriers holding you back." I truly want to inspire.

The *Off the Curb* Dance troupe and our performances became known both nationally and internationally. I served as more than the Director, Choreographer, Business Manager, and Music Producer. I had to make sure that the kids were well taken care of and monitored as we traveled. I also acted and I assisted them as their counselors from time to time as serious issues emerged.

I had such enthusiasm for this group of teens and together we developed into a bit of a phenomenon. I had gone from high school to marriage to becoming a mom and then I founded a creative group for something I loved to do-dance- and we were greatly admired, enjoyed, and respected as professional performers. Although I attended some college, I never lived a college life. I cannot say *Off the Curb* was a surrogate to the college life, but besides feeding my creative spirit, I had fun with the teens and the whole experience. I am a person who sincerely connects with people of all ages. For example, I love playing with my young nephews and nieces and participating in the things they like to do. It brings me pleasure. So with the troupe, often during our off times, I also enjoyed their fun activities as well. Our playful interactions gave me a time to let loose from the pressures associated with the management and performance duties and responsibilities. Their silliness used to drive me crazy but it was also endearing.

Because of the acclaim that both the Dance Troupe and the Outreach Program was gaining, I was asked to teach at a number of different studios and venues. Some of the troupe members took on other duties besides performing because of their level of commitment to *Off the Curb*. They assisted with teaching some of the many after-school groups, an additional skill they gained as a bonus of being a member of the troupe while they earned money for their work. They completed office work, they learned how to set up the sound equipment, and they sold merchandise. In addition, a few members offered suggestions about choreography or performance techniques. I appreciated and valued their creative input, often times using their suggestions. Those dancers felt wonderful and the confidence and self-esteem they built helped to mold them into the adults they are today. Some of the troupe members continue to be involved with my current ventures and have openly and gratefully voiced their opinions about their experience participating in *Off the Curb* with regard to what they gained and learned.

When I reflect back and speak with my past members, I consider what they brought to me as a professional and how they put into action the vision I perceived. For the troupe, I realized I functioned as a combination of a mentor, a mother, an aunt, and a counselor. I took the troupe throughout the United States, Canada, and Europe to perform at various events. These trips exposed the teens to a variety of personalities in the dance world. I never had any formal training in how to choreograph, how to create a dance troupe, or how to advance a dance troupe. I did have the proper instincts and hopped on board any opportunity I had to have the troupe dance. I knew enough to demand that the members dance and behave in a top-notch professional manner. This meant to never stop dancing if something happened to the sound, to thank all those around you that complimented your skills, to be open, to have conversations with audience members, to market the merchandise, and to always put your heart and soul into the performance. My training of the troupe paid off because they became somewhat famous in the hip-hop dance world with many requests for autographs. *Off the Curb* opened for concerts for Missy Elliot, Busta Rhymes, LL Cool J, Outkast, and Lil'Kim to name a few. *Off the Curb* was sponsored by Avia, Phat Farm, Converse, and Reebok and wore their clothing during the shows. They performed at the annual Arthur Ashe Kid's day in Queens, New York among other venues. Most importantly, each member found their true self, they gained confidence, and an appreciation for hard work and commitment. It is no exaggeration to say I had to have a million eyes and that I had to wear a thousand hats and that my mind had to work twenty-four hours a day. I wrote all the grants, networked with clothing companies, made all the bookings, scheduled all the classes, created fundraiser shows, cared for the sound equipment and became the MC. *Off the Curb* was emotionally fulfilling. The dancers are to this day known for their performances and I am often referred to as "The Dance Lady." I was able to take these groups (members changed from time to time due to circumstances) out of Newport to see and experience other environments. That ability was freeing for them as well as educational, especially in understanding the various components of real life.

 In short, I lived and breathed *Off the Curb* and sometimes it brought me to places I had not anticipated. For example, as I had mentioned the kids were asked for autographs following their performances. At the Arthur Ashe event one year, an extended line of children who were carrying extra-large souvenir tennis balls formed and waited to have the dancers autograph them, for two of my young black girls in particular. When I realized what was happening, I approached the girls and the crowd and took them away saying they had to leave. The crowd of youngsters had confused them for Serena Williams and Alexandra Stevenson which seemed humorous at the time, but upon reflection spoke to the underlying racist assumption that black women all look alike. There were other situations as well that were examples of racial profiling or discrimination directed toward teens. One such occasion was when we were enjoying some down time, we were at a hotel and relaxing in a jacuzzi. When one of my young black dancers entered the jacuzzi, with a white family who had also been in there, the mother quickly and anxiously whisked her children out of the jacuzzi. That mother's actions left my dancer feeling as if there was something wrong with him while he shared the relaxing waters with them. Another example was when one of my dancers was waiting to order food on the train and was completely ignored until I politely spoke up that he had been patiently waiting. He was a teen, and the adults were being waited on first. I reference these experiences because they are disturbing and disheartening racist observations that I confronted from time to time in my travels with the dance troupe. It made me see that people can be blatantly racist toward kids of color (and rude to teens). I was able to be supportive and empathetic toward my kids, even though I will never really know what it was like for them, or truly understand how it feels to be treated unfairly due to having brown or black skin. All I could guarantee was that I was a safe person to them and held no judgements. Again, I ensured that in the *Off the Curb* sphere all were accepted, despite the inequalities present in the world. I may never have understood these actions and emotions had my work not brought me in this direction. I gained a great deal of empathy and compassion. I wanted to have kids perform and experience life's joyful escapades. And in the process, I found I also had to protect them from the hurtful actions of some people. I took my position as a "Mentor" seriously and refused to allow these kinds of behaviors to mar the overall positive and joyous experiences that were the greater part of the Dance Troupe. It was important to me that I was aware of and present for all that was occurring with the teens and that they knew they were seen and understood.

The troupe members learned their own unique and individual lessons from the years spent with *Off the Curb*. The lessons included, but were not limited to the development of sophisticated communication skills, tolerating individuals with a variety of personalities, and learning the importance of professionalism. I am grateful for all of the challenges associated with operating *Off the Curb* and the stamina and endurance I attained as well as the lessons I learned. The teens were like sponges soaking in all of the accolades from the audiences and the community, and absorbing the work ethic and life skills I taught them. They learned how to talk things through when difficulties arose. They connected with their creative souls. This unique experience provided a pathway for the many adolescents to grow and mature and work toward becoming the best versions of themselves under my guidance. They probably had little awareness that the combination of fun with work was great preparation for their future adult lives.

Personally, I learned to stay with a given idea until it grew to its best possibility and to never give up in spite of the obstacles. I believed strongly and conveyed this belief to the kids that each show had to be the best version of the performance. We had a specific situation where only four kids could travel to New York for a performance and as proof of the messages I had instilled in the dancers, they danced with every piece of their hearts and souls. They were given a standing ovation at the conclusion of the performance. The old saying that, "the show must go on" was absolutely fulfilled. Understanding the importance and integrating the concept of commitment into their individual value systems and behaviors can never be lost once learned. With that understanding we all became better people. Many conversations have occurred around resurrecting *Off the Curb* always ending with the same conclusion. It cannot be replicated. When the troupe finished its course in 2008, *Off the Curb* was completed. The timing of its existence was perfect and the benefits we all gained were extraordinary. *Off the Curb* prepared us to accept the next phases of our lives because that was what was supposed to be.

The Take-Away:

I never called myself a mentor but realize looking back that in addition to all of the hats I wore in teaching my dance classes, my physical fitness classes, and directing my dance troupe, that I also served as a mentor to many of the teens. Honestly, I did not understand the heaviness of the responsibility I had taken on. I had an acupuncturist take one of my dance classes early on and she told me that I was not only a teacher, but a sensei, identifying that I instill wisdom in the participants while teaching my classes. Like the karate teacher who guides students to use mind energy, I too encourage and direct my students to do the same. I not only wanted the teens to be awesome dancers and performers, I wanted them to be better people. I wanted to teach them the importance of always working with a sense of professionalism as they started to form as a troupe. Additionally, they needed to be caring and thoughtful individuals. My siblings and I were highly influenced by our father who drilled us about the importance of service to others and encouraged us to think about those options as future career paths. My brother served in the military, and my sister was a member of the state police force. I saw myself as a bit of a black sheep being the hip-hop dancer until it occurred to me that I too was in the service of others, through my youth outreach program.

A take-away that I did not anticipate was the amount of time I would need in order to create and maintain cohesion in the group. Each individual teen brought their issues forward and sometimes it meant I had to make time to have a, "We need to talk" session. Although I may have gotten eye rolls, they all respected my leadership and heard me out. I too would listen attentively to them.

Sometimes the issues were sensitive and it took them by surprise that I was calling them on their behaviors. And sometimes their actions interfered with the troupe specifically and I had to suspend them from a performance. These interventions were not always easy, but they were necessary. It conveyed to the troupe that they had a responsibility to the group and to recognizing the effort and commitment needed to have and give top notch performances. Most of the families were supportive and delighted in seeing their child perform. I did have mothers who would help with driving the dancers to events and they were very much appreciated by all. For the after- school program we would have two big performances a year. One in November "Bringing in the Funk" and one in May "School's Out." Both were highly attended with long lines to get in. Those performances were a chance for the after-school kids to perform. Following the after-school performances, the troupe completed the event with a full show of their material.

There was not consistent community support because I don't think hip-hop was considered a respected dance form back then. It was more looked upon as a hangout for kids to have fun. Most people didn't realize what was going on inwardly. I was changing lives. It's hard to communicate with authority the many physical and intellectual skills associated with dance choreography to "lay" people. I also do not think we were appreciated for the artistry which always included cutting edge Choreography, R&B singing, Rapping, and Beat Boxing. The performances were always evolving and never monotonous. The leaders in the Newport community did not seem to take the performances seriously, until I was closing the studio and ending the troupe. They voiced their disappointed feelings when the program and the Dance Troupe were closing, but by then it was too late to change directions. Their sentiments left me with the question, "Where were you?" And, "You want to support me now, but where were you the last sixteen years?" I ended with a bit of cynicism because I felt the community leaders could have stepped up on a number of occasions, but only spoke up at the end to suit their own individual agendas. Feeling this way is unfortunate, but will never diminish all of the benefits, achievements, and pure delight in knowing that I touched souls to improve humanity and those souls in turn touched me so I could continue on a creative course albeit a different one.

Guidance:

If you are going to start a dance company, you have to be absolutely passionate and completely committed. Starting any business requires that you live it twenty-four hours a day, breathing, eating, and sleeping it. You have to select people who have the same mission and vibe as you. You may have to make difficult choices such as removing the best dancer because of negative energy. It is like firing someone. The troupe must be cohesive and the dancers must be respectful of each other and their talents. The group has to respect the leader's decisions although there can be some democratic input. In removing a dancer, there can be a ripple effect on the troupe so the leader has to be ready and adept at resolving issues. Often these conflicts organically took care of themselves.

The job of a mentor is to cultivate and mold somebody to become the best version of him or herself. A mentor must be sincere and authentic. You do not have to be a sweet happy person one hundred present of the time as long as the kids know you care about them. Most people want to hear the truth in a way that makes them a better human. There may come a time when the student is ready to move on and the mentor must encourage this evolution. The student may become the mentor for the next person. Sometimes your student may outshine you because you gave them all the skills they required. That's most assuredly a positive outcome. It is always admirable when the students surpass the teacher. It is like the quote, "Give me a fish and I eat for a day. Teach me to fish and I eat for a lifetime." Give people the skills to be their best selves. This means as the mentor you have to put your ego aside. If you as the mentor want to be better than your students or you do not want to see them excel or rise above you, then mentorship is not for you. I didn't choose mentorship. It evolved naturally. I was living my authentic passion, the life I promoted. It wasn't a reach for me to not use drugs. I wasn't a violent person. I was walking the walk. As a mentor you have to walk that walk and be completely genuine, especially when working with teens. They see right through you. In both instances, being a mentor and creating a business, you do give up some part of your life. Sometimes you do sacrifice a little bit of your own life to make someone else's life a little easier or better.

You have to take risks when you are creating something new. With my dance concepts, I would put them out there and then watch as the kids developed them. I guided them when needed. One of the complications I encountered working with teens was, if they didn't see it on a video, or in a magazine, then in their minds it wasn't cool. I had to make them believe it was cool. That happened quite a bit. However, many times the choreography or concepts they originally thought were uncool would appear in movies or videos about six months later. And they would be amazed. Luckily, I was able to get them to take chances and try new concepts with lots of effort and trust in their creative abilities. They learned along with me that some ideas worked, some did not. I must say, most did and I was always ahead of my time.

You have to believe strong enough in your idea, that your concept will succeed and then you bring it to fruition. As a creative person, sometimes ideas come into your mind and spirit and the vision appears in your own head. But to manifest it and make it happen, you cannot be afraid to fail. You cannot be afraid to look foolish. You cannot be afraid to have people look at you and say,

"What is she doing now?" You have to move forward and take that risk. If the teens did not see one of their hip-hop role models doing what I asked of them in their videos and they opposed it by saying it was goofy I would just say, "We're doing it." Photographer Clint Clemens would photograph the troupe from time to time. One of his images was to have us dressed in our camouflage outfits and pose on a mountain. One of my dancers retorted, "This is not hip-hop." I answered him with, "If Busta Rhymes did it then it would be hip-hop?" I continued, "Hip-hop is who you are. Hip-hop is how you live, hip-hop is the culture. You are hip-hop." Still another time, a young male dancer requested, "Can you make this a boy move?" With that question I answered, "You are a boy, this is the move. How you choose to do the move will make it be a boy move." You have to be strong enough in your belief that your concept and your choreography is that which you envision and demand that the dance be performed as you have demonstrated. You have to be one hundred percent sold on your own idea and completely and passionately step forward. You have to have thick skin knowing you may fail or you may fly. People may laugh or think you are strange or odd. You have to believe enough in your idea that you do not care what people think. I tried different ideas and projects that didn't work and there was some frustration about it not working. You process it and then let it go. But when it does work it is powerful, like a masterpiece, completely artistic leaving you full of gratification.

Part Three

Healer

Chapter 9 -
"More Past, Regrets, Relationships"

To live without regrets is to believe you have nothing to learn, no amends to make, and no opportunity to be braver with your life.

Brene' Brown

      I still feel that I am very much a solo soul. What is interesting about me is that on the weekend my phone never rings. I never receive invitations to socialize, be it dinner, to share a drink, or to even take a walk. No one ever reaches out to me which strikes me as being odd because of all the people that I do know and that I am in contact with on a daily basis over a period of years. Basically, when I finish my work on Fridays and Saturdays, I find myself heading home, alone. On Sundays, I do see my family which is an enjoyable built in routine that gives our family time to visit and catch up. It is our time to watch sports, hang out at the pool, and spend quality time with one another. I have a couple of very close friends with whom I am in daily phone contact, but it does baffle me and I am curious about why I am so isolated. I rationalize being alone because I think most of those around me believe that I am constantly busy. I am always the one that initiates getting together with others if I want to socialize. I don't understand why people don't ask me. It is a weird thing for which I do not have an explanation.

I am not lonely because ironically my life is full with my work, friends, and family. The conflict is that I would love to have a romantic partner but I also enjoy the simplicity of my single life. I don't have to cook for someone, I don't have to share the remote, or compromise. But I don't have that person at the end of the day to talk to about my accomplishments, problems, or concerns. I'm fine with my lifestyle most of the time. I am comfortable with myself, but it would be nice to have a special person to share my time with to do things together on the weekends and other times. I have not really experienced a long-term healthy, happy, and romantic relationship. It is difficult knowing how to open myself up to meeting compatible men. I feel as though when I do venture out, I leave myself open to socializing. But I have the impression that people do not see me for who I truly am. They do not see my spirit. I have reached the conclusion that if a relationship is supposed to happen it is going to happen. I am leaving it to the universe.

I have tried what most single individuals have tried with regard to dating sites. But I must say I don't have the energy to stay on the dating sites for prolonged periods of time. And I have not been one to power date. I feel as though I do not need a relationship so badly that I have to tolerate a bunch of bad dates before I find a decent one. This leads me to believe that perhaps, I really do not want to be committed to one person. Many of my closest friends are gay and in relationships, and I do spend time socializing with them. I have a couple of friends who are single with whom I should probably spend more time. When I have shared with others about my isolation, I do get surprised reactions, but nothing seems to change. I suppose that I am not an easy person to be matched up with, or that I do not care enough to put effort into finding the just right man. I think others may want me involved with a partner more than I want the connection myself. What I do know, is that I have tried it all-attending fundraisers or events, dating apps, and putting myself out there. Discussing the finding of a mate is the conversation that goes nowhere. My early life experiences must be playing a part somewhere deep within my soul as unresolved issues or maybe the solo-soul part of me is perfectly content.

For the most part, I am comfortable in my own skin, although as I profess I too am continually striving to become the best version of myself. I maintain a healthy lifestyle and practice what I preach. I spend thirty minutes each morning in grounding myself spiritually and readying myself for the day by using meditation, journaling, and stating my affirmations. I undergo therapy, listen to podcasts that expand my mind and keep me positive. I continue to keep learning and studying about human behavior while trying to apply the skills I have learned to my daily functioning. I like to abide by Maya Angelou's saying, "when you know better, you do better." To that end, seeing a therapist (which all therapists generally do) assists me in figuring out how to work on those attributes about myself that I wish to change or improve. Healing and growing spiritually is an everyday process which requires a concerted commitment to the work.

Even though I understand human nature, the pitfalls in relationships, not just romantic ones, can be confusing and hurtful. Being in the business of physical fitness certainly has its positive and fulfilling successes. But what may not be totally apparent to observers are the sensitive and not so obvious issues that may arise in my interactions with clients. Those relationships are very important to me. In my role, I have to be completely attentive to my participants, noticing their skill levels as well as understanding their personality traits. I keep my classes upbeat, with lots of motivational encouragement mixed in with my sarcastic sense of humor. Physical fitness is connected to body image and involves mental energy. As the trainer I am held to a higher standard and sometimes seen as "super human." Some clients expect me to intuitively know their individual personal needs beyond fitness, which is unrealistic and can sometimes make me a target for their inability to address those needs on their own. They often project those issues on me as if the trainer can fix everything. My studio is an environment of positive energy with lots of camaraderie among the clients. Finding the balance to be accommodating to all during the hour- long classes is sometimes challenging.

However, I always make sure that I am attentive to each person, even if I must make quick eye contact to ensure the person I will be right there. The difficulty is, when a client wants more of their fair share and becomes accusatory, implying that I have broken some kind of trust. It may be surprising to read about such behaviors, but I think it is of interest to point out in light of the theme of my story. It is human nature to sometimes misunderstand communications because each individual views their personal issues through their own perspective. Those perspectives can be skewed because of their own unresolved struggles. They become distorted according to their internal narratives which can be negative because of their present state of mind. In any case, to make quick judgments, especially for those who have had long term affiliations with me, is unfair. I, of course, take criticism seriously because of both the impact toward my professional reputation and because I do not want to be hurtful. I check myself with those that I trust and can confide in about my communications and actions to make sure that I am fair and professionally responsible. I always reach out to understand and/or to mend situations as they may arise. It is crucial that I maintain an open and positive environment in my studio because I sincerely care about each client. When I mentioned that I created a safe and all-inclusive atmosphere early on in my career with *Off the Curb*, my essence has remained the same throughout all of my endeavors. However, if at some point, there is not a way to reach a mutual resolution, then it becomes necessary to let go, move on, and learn from those interactions. I like to think everything in life happens for a reason or doesn't happen for a reason. And I am extraordinarily grateful that those uneasy interactions seldom occur. Nevertheless, I attribute the inability to find an agreeable solution as an unfortunate occurrence that will happen sporadically. Making me the target is an indication that the client was going through their own difficulties, and I must simply accept those decisions.

We all have regrets in life. Those regrets, mistakes, unforeseen turn of events provide us lessons that if we reflect on will become integrated into our minds when making future choices. If we consider those actions from this perspective, then we can view them as purposeful in improving our lives. Much better to find the lesson as opposed to harboring the turmoil and wishing we had taken a different route. Still, I always wondered what it would have been like if I had stayed in California and not come back because I was doing so well. What would life have been like if I stayed a bit longer? I will never know. I made the decision to follow the person I loved. I thought it was the right thing to do toward the next stage of developing a relationship.

I cannot say it was a huge regret in retrospect because shortly after I returned back to the east, I created *Off the Curb*. I used the inspiration I found in California, honed my skills, and decided to implement my vision. However, I do wish I had more business savvy when I operated *Off the Curb* because I could have created more of a structure so the organization could have perpetuated. *Off the Curb* was me winging it. Once I was finished managing the dance troupe, there was not a willing person to continue its existence because I had no blueprint to follow and expand on the vision. It wasn't an organized business. It was me doing what I do. Yet, the relationships made and developed live on forever as does my desire to use my creativity.

I regret not seeing my father's hopelessness and not having the knowledge I have now when my father was going through his ordeal. Could I have helped him or prevented his suicide? Looking back, I realize now there were plenty of red flags. By undergoing such an incredibly powerful loss, I found my way toward the counseling profession. I saw that I had a personal experience knowing how deep the darkness of grief can be. And from this position, I knew I could help others find their way through the dark night of the soul. I knew I had become very adept at helping others through the grieving process, understanding how deep the pain can grab hold of the body and soul.

I regret giving my husband joint custody because my son had the freedom to drink and party while he was a high school kid. I would never have allowed that much leeway for him. However, joint custody bolstered his relationship with his father. Our son had the benefit of knowing he was deeply loved by both of his parents, and we were equal partners in loving him. My son and I are more apt to have open discussions around my fears as he travels toward his goals. I try to stay aware of his needs and I am available to advise and support him when he requests it.

I regret ever going on that walk with the "elusive" man mentioned in an earlier chapter. I knew enough to say "no" to his initial invitation sensing that getting involved with him would be a mistake. But I gave in. The pattern I established with him, which I am sorry to say lasted for years, was to go through phases of seeing or communicating with him intermittently. Our interactions were not based on a commitment for one another and were always ambiguous and inconsistent. There were phases of complete absence or random texts or calls. Even though I regret that walk, my involvement with him taught me a number of hard but important lessons. I learned about human behavior, personality disorders, and what the feeling of addiction can be. I can relate to people who have addictions because that is what my involvement with him felt like. I have reached a point where I can say that our pseudo relationship is over.

When I closed *Off the Curb*, I stopped my life for a little while. I was truly at a stand-still and needed time to sort through all that I had been through. In fact, I had come through both an incredible "high" having experienced all of the benefits associated with living in the performance world receiving all sorts of audience praise and celebrated press. Simultaneously, I had been through and was in the midst of an extreme "low" processing those years that held the sadness of losing my father and trying to recover from that tragedy. I had gone through a divorce, which was a complete lifestyle change involving sharing my son which felt as though I had lost him since I was not with him every day. Top those extremes with the chaos of total confusion and blankness of mind and spirit in trying to figure out what I was going to do next professionally, and it is easy to understand how "falling apart" or "hibernating" could become viable options. I think many people in this state of mind are apt to find ways to self-medicate or withdraw in other ways because of the difficulty of being in the "no direction" zone. I could have very easily been that person. But, I had the wherewithal and the strong will to remain hopeful for my next phase because I wanted to be a successful role-model for my son. I literally gave myself permission to pause and allowed myself time to breathe while I did deep soul reflection. I began to study the inspirational work of Tony Robbins who I can best describe as an empathetic guru as well as a financial genius. He encourages those who he coaches to empower themselves with self-improvement skills. He has written a number of books and hosts inspirational, educational conferences. His body of work helped formulate my decision to study human behavior and to finally complete my undergraduate Psychology Degree. I accomplished this goal through an online program and then attended a Graduate Program in Holistic Mental Health Counseling.

The process of earning my degrees was not a clear cut one because answers to life's dilemmas are not always obvious. It is acceptable to wait for "divine inspiration." So, while I lived in this holding pattern, I continued to teach fitness classes to pay my bills as my entrepreneurial spirit percolated underground. During this time frame, I began to seriously think about moving to New York. My son was in college and doing well and there was nothing to keep me here. Living in New York was something I had always dreamed of. I decided I would only move if I had a full-time job and a decent place to live. I found New York City's vibrancy to be inspirational and energizing. While working with *Off the Curb* I had traveled to New York to take classes honing my dance skills that further enhanced the quality of the productions. Toward the end of the *Off the Curb's* existence as a dance troupe, I would go to New York for half of the week and teach classes and return to Rhode Island for the other half of the week. Spending time in New York City was more than a change of scenery and a place to work part-time. In New York, I felt alive. There, I felt I was seen for who I was and am. The New York City dance community consisted of a variety of creative individuals from whom I had lots to learn. Eventually, a job opportunity did present itself at the New York Sports Club on the upper east side as a fitness manager. I was led to believe that I was perfectly qualified for the position and that I had a good chance that I would be hired. However, that did not turn out to be the case. Instead the company decided to hire from within and I was left disappointed and deflated. My hopes had been squashed and I had to move to my plan B after spending a solid six weeks going through an interview process. My sister had offered to assist me financially so I could go follow through on my dream to move to New York. I so appreciated her support and generosity. She understood how I had thrived being in New York.

I found out later the New York Sports Club would not have been a good fit anyway. It was not suitable for my skills and pursuits because it was too corporate, and did not allow or encourage creativity. It would have been a position that would have supported a move to New York, but it would have smothered my creative spirit and probably would have made me miserable. I learned later that not working for the Sports Club was actually the universe taking care of me. I remained adamant that I didn't want to move to New York without some sort of plan, even though in my heart and soul I knew New York City had the options I was looking for in my next career move, for my freedom, and for my energy. I just did not have it in me to stay there without some stability. I had been so deeply disappointed, I could not muster up the effort needed to institute a Plan B in New York.

My next career move took place back home on Aquidneck Island. I felt it was time to operate a studio again. The operation would be under my own parameters which had served me well throughout my time with *Off the Curb*. I had no qualms about jumping in, although I was not a hundred percent sure how this next manifestation would congeal. I had the idea for developing able-minded bodies, which seemed to emerge from out of nowhere. That is how my mind seems to work, just like in childhood when I would create stories in my mind. I select what I want the outcome to be. My faith in the universe guided me toward implementing the ideas in my head. I was not a person who would succumb to inert emotions brought on by disappointments or failures. I knew I had connections on

Aquidneck Island. I thought I could do life coaching as a friend had suggested, telling me I "was easy on the soul." And I knew I could run fitness and dance classes. The idea for *Able Body and Mind* materialized and within six weeks I opened my studio in Middletown RI. I created a community of members who had a lot of fun together and enjoyed great camaraderie. I had members who loved very strenuous, kick-ass workouts as well as those who loved dance. Some members went to Vermont and participated in the "Tough Mudder" together, while other members enjoyed dancing in performances. I invited guest teachers and we performed flash mobs. I used great sayings with a play on the word "Able" like: "We are unstoppAble," and "We are unbreakAble" to go along with the performances. We often went out to dinner together to celebrate our work. I had created such an amazing community and I truly felt I had answered my next calling. As a side note, while I operated my studio, I had also begun taking classes at Salve Regina University to complete my degree in Holistic Counseling to which I previously referred. I do have one more regret that had to do with the *Able Body and Mind* studio. We had built such a strong community, but the studio was suffering financially and I chose to close the business. In hindsight, I wish that I had sat down and had a conversation with the members to discuss the financial difficulties that I began to experience. I think if I had told them about these struggles, they probably would have offered to help. The lesson here is to value my work and allow myself to rely on my community.

It is difficult to identify the sequence of how my life moved from struggling to figure out what to do after *Off the Curb*, to attempting to make a firm and committed move to New York City, to the opening and closing of *Able Body and Mind* without addressing what was underlying those decisions. And that has to do with my resistance in believing that I deserve abundance, including financial abundance. Somewhere along the line, I internalized the belief that I didn't deserve to be lucrative. I had the core belief that I didn't deserve to have everything I wanted. This realization and insight became apparent through therapy. I was introduced to Hakomi therapy during my studies at Salve. It is a form of therapy which uses a series of statements as probes and little experiments to connect the client's narrative with body sensations. The body has an organic reaction in response to a statement that evokes a feeling before the mind intellectualizes it. As open as I am to taking creative risks, I am just as open to exploring those aspects of my personality that prompt me to formulate choices. I became curious about Hakomi and wanted to break this core belief. Therefore, I saw a therapist for six months to help me break down this issue. I wanted to address and place past insecurities into their proper perspectives so they would not interfere with my ability to make present day decisions.

With assistance, I learned that I was holding on to a belief system that I should live with basically enough to get by. That's all I should have. Growing up we never had more than enough. We had just what we needed like one pair of sneakers for the whole school year. We were a middle-class family and my father did not strive to accumulate more and more just to have lots of valuable things. We just always maintained what we had. Contrary to my father, my husband was interested in making lots of money and wanted an abundance of things. Because my husband was focused on financial security and abundance, I never had to think about this part of our marriage. His concentration on finances enabled me to pursue the things I wanted to do. I never had to deal with my core beliefs around finances until it became a challenge and I was on my own, after our divorce. How was I going to make money? How was I going to become independently financially secure? He had made sure that my son and I were financially secure when we initially divorced, buying the furniture for my apartment because he wanted to make sure that our son had all the nice things he needed in both households. He paid for everything. I did not pass on my core belief to our son. He has enough of his father's influence to know that he is deserving of the things he wants and to go after them.

    I finally incorporated into my being that I could have everything I wanted after much soul searching and have concluded it is fine to want more than just enough. I want financial freedom to travel, and to have those things that bring me pleasure and peace. I understand that the feeling of "not deserving" can manifest itself in surprising ways, and I want to value the work I do by being fully compensated for the expertise of my skills. It is still a dream to live in New York City and have an apartment there. It would be wonderful to be able to do my work in both environments. I think the difference between Aquidneck Island and New York City is the fact that there is room for all kinds of people and programs in the city. Competition is not looked upon as threatening, but more as the chance to offer alternatives while also learning from various professionals.

The Take-Away:

Here I further confess my mistakes and the lessons I learned as a result. There is no question that it is hard to face up to mistakes and reflect about them. But once you practice the skill to be most honest with yourself it is such a relief, unloading a burden or burdens. Mohammed Ali says, "If you are the same man at fifty that you were at twenty, then you have wasted thirty years." Having regrets about not following your instincts or intuitions is a natural attribute of human behavior and is not to be voraciously obsessed about. It should be given its due attention and then placed in a part of your intellect that reminds you to not make the same mistake, or to avoid situations that bring you to destructive places. Every decision I have made, every relationship I was in, every person I met, and every person I froze in front of were all lessons to teach me about myself and to help me grow and become a more evolved and deeper person. I had to have those life experiences to learn the lessons I needed to continue my travels along life's path. My goal in life is to become the best version of myself. If I never stopped to think about the choices I made and how they benefited or hurt me, then it is impossible to learn to appreciate and have gratitude toward them. Although I might not have made the same decisions now as a more evolved individual, all of my decisions led me to where I am. So, for that I cannot fully regret all of them. There is always a curiosity, which is a healthy way to approach self- reflection. Asking the questions- "What if I tried this? Or that?" I can't dwell on the "what ifs" and I can't be bitter over the past even if the past was horrible. If I let myself become bitter, then I become a victim or enmeshed in the past and can never move forward. I remain stuck and that is not in my nature.

It bears repeating that with my son, I wish I could have been more of an influence so he would not have had so much freedom to be drinking and partying during high school. But on the other side of it, he and his father became much closer and his father was more involved in his life, paying attention to all that he was doing without me being the only one in charge. Becoming a better father, made him a better person. I regret part of my decision of joint custody, but if I look at the lesson in all of it, it was a pretty positive lesson. Even though for me it was so difficult to be away from my son. If you look at my son now, he is a combination of both mine and his dad traits - the good and the bad. We were married really young and did not really know what we were getting into. Yet, I do not fully regret our marriage because my ex-husband and I had lots of fun together. We traveled to California, and we had our beautiful son.

Again, I do wish I had created an organizational structure and that I had better business sense so someone could have stepped in to take over *Off the Curb*. I wish I knew the value of my work with both *Off the Curb* and with the *Able, Body, and Mind* Studio. If I knew and believed in my value, both enterprises would have been financially successful as well as personal successes. In both circumstances I created community experiences that brought individuals together in positive activities and events that were enjoyable opportunities for personal gains and improvements. Finding myself in financial difficulty taught me to value myself and never underestimate my worth. That does not mean I don't struggle presently with this issue, but I have learned that the quality of the work I offer is worth it to the participants who choose to partake. Do I wish I understood this point then? Of course. There is a recurrent saying about "wishing I knew then what I know now." But I learned the lesson. If you do not learn the lesson you are just going to repeat the mistake over and over.

After I was divorced I waited for a while before I started to date. My son was graduating from high school and I didn't want to disrupt the focus on him. When I did start my relationship with "the elusive man" he was actually a good fit for my lifestyle at the time. It is not like I wanted someone all the time but I got what I needed spending time with him. He fulfilled a need for me. Regretfully, I have always been attracted to bad boys. I blame it on "Fonzie" from *Happy Days*. I blame it on Beau Brady from "Days of Our Lives." I blame it on John Travolta from "Grease." In all those fictional instances they made the bad boy have a good heart. The bad boy always did the right thing at the end. They were glamorized. My father was a bad boy. My husband was a bad boy. It does make sense that I picked "this elusive man" because he fits my "old" pattern. As a therapist, I know he is the type of person who should be a client rather than a partner and as a result of my time with him I learned more about human behavior. I have learned what I don't want in a partner and am ready for who I do want. And to my credit, I didn't raise a bad boy, I raised a good man in my son.

Guidance:

When I work with clients, I encourage them to look at their lives and do a fearless moral inventory. This is a practice of Twelve Step Programs and is required of its participants. It means looking at our lives honestly including all of the good and the bad and identifying our role in each situation. It holds us accountable and responsible for past and present behaviors. This is a good place to begin in self-reflection and it doesn't matter what age you are. Each of us spends time every day making thousands of choices, some more significant than others. They range on a spectrum from thinking about the things we say to how we treat others. All of those choices impact us in one way or another, either bringing us joy or stress or something in between. And if an individual is stable and content, then maybe that person is doing the things that are right for their individual self. If on the other hand, the person is in a constant state of depression or anxiety, without the presence of a life altering event, then perhaps that person should figure out why he or she is so unhappy. The Fearless Moral Inventory is never all negative. We celebrate the good as well.

I ask the individual to evaluate all of the decisions that s/he made and to identify the things that were done well and then identify those that could have done better. Finally, the person can hopefully accept who they are. Acknowledge who you are with the mixture of the good and the not so good. By bringing to light all the good things about oneself and all the things you could have done better sets the person free. If there is someone that you hurt along the way, you attempt to make amends. It is important to acknowledge your shortcomings. Most people do not want to acknowledge them and instead hide from them. But if you can acknowledge your shortcomings or wrongdoings and make amends for them, then they lose their power and cannot hurt you anymore. What we don't face and heal can become pain bodies within us that are easily triggered when stressed. We are never fully transparent because we are always hiding.

When apologizing to those you may have hurt remember, they do not have to accept your apology. But in order for you to heal you have to say the words aloud, whether in person or through writing. In some cases, you may never be able to say this directly to the person aloud or in writing. You may not have the opportunity or it may not be safe. There are many reasons why the apology allows healing for you but you have to allow the other person to have their feelings. Perhaps, they will start to heal from your acknowledgement and apology and with time may be able to create a healing relationship with you or they may not. Most importantly, depending on the severity of the problems and/or abuse, you may want to do this healing work with professional support or with a sponsor. A therapist can guide you through the painful process, especially if you do not get the response you want.

In our reflective states, if we can get curious about the choices we make and begin to ask questions, the answers help to teach us how to make better decisions moving forward. We may want to ask:
- What did that decision teach me?
- What kind of success do I deserve?
- What kind of person do I want to spend my life with?
- What kind of people do I want to associate with?
- What kind of job do I want?

- What do I hope to accomplish in life?
- How important is financial security to me?

If your curiosity is genuine, you will learn and not keep repeating the same mistakes and behaviors and grow and evolve toward your best self. Otherwise, you remain in the same place and perpetuate your existence without reflection. You may become bitter and tend to blame others.

Something that is often neglected or we fail to think about is how crucial self-care practices are to our mental and physical well-being. Self-care practices are meant to ground an individual. Someone who has experienced trauma, anxiety or depression will benefit from grounding practices, techniques, and tools. Their emotional waves can be very low, or high and low, or they are living in a constant panic state. Self-care can help them establish a pathway into a state of equilibrium. Creating a regular routine for exercise falls under the self-care practice options. Very often, those who are suffering internally are in a fight or flight mode so the exercise allows the energy and adrenaline to be used in a healthy way. While exercising, endorphins are hormones that are released, improving and raising the level of your mood. If you have been traumatized those feelings can be held in your body and through exercise you can move through to get to the other side of trauma. Emotional support, I have termed as *Mental Fitness* helps to reframe how you see things.

Chapter 10 - "Manifesting Dreams"

Love thy soul, manifest thy light.

Lallah Gifty Akita

I've always had the power to manifest. Manifesting is visualizing the completion of something a person wants to achieve, possess or have happen in life. I have a number of examples where I have manifested successfully, but I also struggle with personal impediments that only allow me to go so far. I become constricted in crossing over. The not being able to cross over is what I do not understand about myself and I am in a perpetual battle to find reasons. It is one of my on-going self-examination projects. I inch my way toward a dream but I never fully reach it. I could say this idea of visualizing started as far back as when I had my paper route dreams as a kid. I was eleven years old and I always had this vision of being in a bigger life, like being in Hollywood, traveling the world, and being on tour with rock bands. I always felt like I was destined for more and deep down in my soul that my life was meant for major achievements. I believed I was going to become famous. I spoke about my childhood earlier and how I felt alone but could escape into my creative mind. I would sit on the porch and play Kenny Rogers music and like most little girls, believed that Prince Charming was coming to save me from the mundane existence I lived. It wasn't that I hated my life, my family, or my friends. There was a consistent nudging in my soul that was seeking other adventures, and it reverberated a feeling inside that there had to be more to life than just this ordinary routine. My great aunt, my grandmother's sister always told me I belonged in Hollywood. I did make it there, but I didn't stay. Interestingly, often times in life those around you may sense a gift inside of you that you do not necessarily see in yourself. But reflecting back, I think it was intuitive of my great aunt to know this dream lived inside of me.

When I won Miss Teen Rhode Island and I met childhood stars, it was an amazing accomplishment that gave me my first peek into the world of fame. Those stars took pictures with me as much as I was taking pictures with them. They were surrounded by beauty queens which certainly created an impressive photo opportunity. Their careers were enhanced surrounded by idols from a different category other than that of the acting profession. The irony was that we were both kids. They were the movie stars and naturally we were grateful to be in their company. But truthfully, both groups were charmed with one another. I never realized that this meeting was a reciprocated experience during the time it actually occurred. Only after the fact, as I reflect back to my childhood did I understand the situation in which I found myself. I happened to act on one of my instincts, entering the beauty contest without looking for any guidance from the adults in my life. With my success winning the contest, I considered myself to be a background participant in a foreign world of stardom. They were the famous actors and I was a small- town girl from Rhode Island. However, for that moment in time as beauty queens, we too were "stars" in our own right. That unexpected encounter with famous people lit a spark in me. The seeds were planted to pursue the life of glamour and excitement.

My dream evolved as I grew older leading me to enter into the fitness world and later the dance world. I took fitness classes from the early age of fourteen and I began teaching fitness when I was eighteen. I did the Jane Fonda workouts from the albums and VHS tapes she had created and enjoyed the exercise and challenges posed by them. I inherited my love for exercise from my father, who as a gymnast, loved physical fitness. To that end, I attended a class given by Karen Voight in Boston one of the top gurus in the fitness world. She offered a Master Class and I attended it. Upon attending this workshop, I immediately felt enamored by her teaching style and wanted to exemplify it. She was the first fitness instructor that I saw that I was really amazed by and I knew I had the ability and talent to become as skilled as she. I had been inspired and I began to work toward emulating her but with my own expressive style. With my eventual move to California, where Karen's famous studio was based, I was able to manifest that dream and work for her. It turned out to be an experience of a lifetime. It was surreal and I couldn't believe I was actually in this world that catered to famous people. In my work at the studio, with my energy and skills developing, I slowly became well known. I was invited to teach during the more popular time slots.

Among the famous talent that frequented the studio, one particular day, I met Paula Abdul. We were both at the studio café and chatted with one another. When she commented that she should take one of my classes, I must admit I froze. I thought why is this famous choreographer (at that time she was Janet Jackson's choreographer as well as making her own music videos) talking to me and wanting to take my class? There was something in me that couldn't accept this admiration and literally I had no words to respond to her. I did not feel I was worthy to be in the same company as this star. I was an unknown trainer from the smallest state in the United States that had no specific resume to pull upon. That core belief that I was a "nobody" resurfaced. I cannot articulate why I felt this way at the time, because the reality was I did have real talent. All I know is that I shut down, and she probably thought I was a loon because I just stopped talking. In hindsight, I realized we were about the same age, she was only two years older than me, and we could have been friends. We could have hung out. I could have stepped into her world very easily. Yet, something in my soul and spirit made me believe that she was on a different level and I didn't belong there. At this point I was shy, though motivated and confident in my talents. The opportunity to work with celebrities was a realistic gateway toward a very lucrative career in physical fitness. Something lodged deep within my soul was not letting me accept that I was moving toward that career path. It was strange.

My brush with fame did not end with Karen Voight. I returned to Newport, RI after my work with Karen Voight and created *Off the Curb*. With a tremendous amount of energy and determination, I hustled to get our Dance Troupe into a number of venues, manifesting the troupe as more than a local phenomenon. As a result, we opened concerts for famous hip-hop artists including: Missy

Elliot, Busta Rhymes, LL Cool J, Outkast, and Lil' Kim to name a few. And again, I was in the presence of fame, this time with my dancers. We congregated and socialized together with the artists backstage. I was the onlooker even though I was in the same performance world as these well-known hip-hop artists. Something stopped me from fully crossing over into their world, stopped me from envisioning myself to be on par with the famous. I was committed to my dance troupe but it was highly probable that I could have entered the next level of discovery, if I had so chosen. The responsibility was on me. In fact, Missy Elliot was my age and I certainly could have initiated a conversation both socially and for networking purposes to advance my goals further. I met her when she was a rising star and I was a rising choreographer working with a group of kids. That same feeling arose, that prohibited me from believing that I could be in this famous world because I was an unknown young woman from an insignificant place. That feeling was unconscious but real and intrusive.

I scheduled performances for *Off the Curb* in New York City knowing the exposure that would result from these trips, being among the troupes in one of the international hubs of the Dance World. In my work with dance, I fell in love with Savion Glover's work, considered the world's best tap dancer, and attended his performance with my cousin at the Broadway Show *Bring in 'Da Noise, Bring in 'Da Funk*. We were fortunate to have front row center seats and as I looked up, I felt his soul touching my soul. Savion was all heart when he danced. I wanted to show his powerful moves to my dancers and brought them to a show. I was so inspired and loved his work that I also brought my son and members of my family to his shows. I was determined to connect with him. One of our times in New York City the Troupe I brought my troupe to see Savion's show. While there, as he entered the theater and we handed him *Off the Curb* brochures and merchandise. I had a quick interchange with Savion with the intention of describing my program as briefly as possible. I let him know about the group, how it was founded on promoting no drugs or violence while providing teens with a creative outlet for which to use their time productively. Eventually, I was able to bring him to Newport to do a master class which was huge. I spread the word that Savion Glover would be teaching at my studio and within hours my voicemail was flooded with hundreds of messages. He was definitely at star level. In preparing for his arrival, he had many requests which I tried to honor. My studio was of course filled to capacity when he taught the class. Having Savion Glover in my studio for this class was not a common place occurrence for Newport or for me. It took lots of planning and logistics to make it happen and I was left once more in the outsider position, never crossing over into that star world. A couple of years later, he performed in Providence at PPAC (Providence Performing Arts Center) which the Troupe attended. We gave him a "goodie bag" filled with all sorts of *Off the Curb* merchandise including a t-shirt. To our delight after the intermission Savion wore the *Off the Curb* t-shirt for the second half of the show. The dancers and I were thrilled to see his recognition and acknowledgement of our troupe.

  As I traveled back and forth to New York City, I became ingrained in the city culture, so different from the small island culture of Aquidneck Island. The energy of the city was hard to ignore, especially because as an artist in any capacity the creative opportunities surround you everywhere. And too, there are the diehard New York Yankee fans of which I became, with Derek Jeter as my favorite player. Of course, I manifested meeting him. I had much respect for him as a player for being one who sought to give back to the community that gave him so much acclaim and financial abundance. He has a foundation called "Turn 2" which creates and oversees programs to help teens to turn towards a healthy and productive lifestyle. I volunteered for Jeter's foundation teaching hip- hop to kids in Harlem as an after-school program. I loved this opportunity. The teens accepted me with enthusiasm and that felt good. At the end of the year as an appreciation for the work of the volunteers, the organization invited us to attend a game in one of the box suites at Yankee Stadium. A "Meet and Greet" with Derek Jeter was included as one of the perks, and my manifestation was realized. I ended up spending the whole game with Mrs. Jeter, (Derek's mother) who was amiable and fun. We had great conversations and interactions. I shared with her the details of my work with *Off the Curb* and appreciated hearing them. It just so happened that on that day I had an evening wedding to attend and I was squeezed for time. When the game ended and Derek Jeter arrived to meet us, she took my hand and brought me right to him and introduced me to Derek herself. How exciting was that? My communication with his mother did not continue, but I did send Dr. Jeter, Chairperson of the "Turn 2" Foundation and Derek's father, a copy of my documentary that followed my work with *Off the* Curb. He let me know that he really enjoyed it.

    I found myself having other interactions with famous people. My next story begins with when my cousins were going out to

California to see the *Ellen Show*. They asked me to join them. At the time I greatly admired Kiefer Sutherland from the show "24." I decided I would take the trip in the hopes that I would be able to meet him. This was all in good fun and I considered it an adventure "in search of Kiefer Sutherland." I knew what his hobbies were and where he liked to hang out. I knew I had the power to manifest things and I did meet Kiefer Sutherland in quite an interesting manner. I had gone to see a documentary on the evolution of Kiefer Sutherland's band, "Rocco Deluca and the Burden." The film's title was *I Trust you to Kill Me*. A question and answer period with Sutherland followed the airing of the film, and that was my true purpose for attending. As I sat myself down, more toward the back, I struck up a conversation with the gentleman who was seated beside me. He identified himself as being the band's manager and offered me the option to attend a VIP after show party which I gladly accepted. He gave me the address to the Hollywood Boulevard night club where the party was being held. When I arrived he greeted me, gave me a VIP bracelet, and said to have a good time. Then, he disappeared. I was able to meet Kiefer and saw many of his celebrity friends. However, I remained at the party as an onlooker. I was in awe of all who were there, but at the same time I did not feel that I fit in to this group. Kiefer was "wild" which he is known for and that is just not who I am. I fulfilled my desire to meet him first hand.

These descriptions of standing in the doorway into the world of "stardom" led me toward some soul searching. Why didn't I cross over into that world? I had so many opportunities. It wasn't that I was far away. I was backstage with celebrities, in VIP areas, being introduced (by their mother on a select occasion) to famous athletes, and having performers in my studio. I never felt like I was one of them. I was on the fan side. In the last few years I have been thinking, "Why is my life not bigger than it is?" I reach and inspire many people on a local level. I had opportunities to be on the national and international level if I allowed myself to cross over into the world of the well-known stars who I had met. I don't know if it wasn't my time. My spirit, mind, emotions weren't ready? Did I not have enough life experience yet? I am not sure of the reasons why, but there was an energetic holding back that was within me that kept me from feeling that I deserved that world. I am still working to resolve this. I am a work in progress, figuring out why I often felt less than.

I have learned much about the "star" scene and have found some aspects to be necessary, and other aspects at times not so pleasant. When you reach a certain level of notoriety, you have license to exert your star power, showing that you are not just a regular person. For example, Savion Glover has been a star since childhood, having danced on *Sesame Street* and continuing to develop his talent as an adult. His accomplishments are amazing and like other stars he has earned the rights to adulation by a strong fan base. When he visited my studio, I witnessed first- hand how difficult it can be to meet the very specific demands of a famous person. I will refrain from sharing all of the nitty-gritty details. Certainly, there are several famous individuals who have succumbed to the pressures of their fame because of their constant exposure and unrelenting fan attention. I am sure it can be exhausting and overwhelming. As a result, they can and do develop a hardened outer shell that is filled with entitlement to make these specific demands, perhaps to cope with the pressures of stardom. It is a difficult balancing act to assert your power while remaining professionally respectful. For years, *Off the Curb* performed at the East Coast Alliance in Manhattan at the Marriot Marquee always doing what the Conference Management asked. We respectfully, kindly, and patiently waited for our turn to perform. As the CEO of the troupe, I was never demanding, and was always professional and polite. I finally reached a breaking point because there was much appreciation for our work from conference attendees, yet we received no perks for our extraordinary efforts or support for the program from the conference managers. At one point after feeling dismissed, I decided that for our next performance, we would do our performance and leave right away in "diva" style which is unlike me. I was tired of being polite and not being appreciated for our efforts. We took our "diva" leave and did succeed in getting the manager's attention. The conference attendees loved watching my dancers and the energy they brought energized the other groups. Our exit was definitely noticed. The next day the organizer of the event called me to assure me that for the following year, they would be providing funding for our room and board. The appreciation for our work had been given, once I exhibited some backbone.

My observation of the world of fame was that the talent needed to display diva status in order to gain respect, a whole other level with which I was unfamiliar. I quickly understood it, when placed in the position to demand that respect which we most assuredly deserved. Furthermore, I realized if I wanted to manifest a dream of becoming famous, I have to flesh out those attributes of my dream in order to make it attainable. Is it to be famous or do I want to be able to walk in and out of this world as I please? The world of fame is extreme. You give up a lot and it demands a lot. There is no question that for some individuals it is not in their nature to let go of their "niceness." Not surprisingly, some artists that are at the most extreme have lots of pain underneath their hard or jovial exteriors and creativity becomes their outlet for release and expression. Certainly, some performers use their expertise and skills to mask their deep-seated pain. However, other performers and artists have the capacity to face their issues in spite of being in the limelight. The "world of fame" can be a complicated place and perhaps requires much self-reflection as you approach it. You must build tough skin. You have to know going into that world that you are going to be absolutely adored and torn apart simultaneously.

In reflecting back to all that I have experienced with famous people, I think I was not sure about where I stood. Maybe there was a part of me that didn't know that I could just step in. I was so fixated on the work I was completing- the organization, the choreography, the classes that I didn't take the time to pause. I didn't realize the whole world was open to me. I was a product of small-town thinking not truly manifesting myself on a higher platform. I had gone to both New York City and Hollywood, but then I returned home. When I was twenty-five, I thought my dance career was over so I gave the stage over to the kids. I wanted them to have their turn in rising to fame. Yet looking back, I realized that twenty-five was the prime age for dancers. Maybe dancing was not my calling at the time. Perhaps instead my calling at that time was to be a mentor to young dancers. It would have been fun and an adventure to have entered the celebrity life. I would have welcomed it. The fact that I did not actively pursue the connections I made was somewhat frustrating at the time. Looking back, I see that I had an energetic connection to family and "home" while desiring more. At the same time, I consider myself successful and enjoy my life.

The core belief that I did not belong in the famous arena is curious -freezing up and becoming star struck. I am starting to understand where this core belief began and am currently doing the work to release it.

The Take-Away:

I know that I have had a good life living on the fringes of greatness and, overall, I don't feel like I missed out on huge opportunities. In fact, I appreciate all of it. But the curiosity remains regarding my hesitation to step into fame. Apparently, the universe led me on the paths I was destined to follow, perhaps in preparation for this next phase of my life for which I am ready to move forward. I was compelled to go down all those paths and then found myself at a "manifest standstill" just for a brief moment in time. With all the years of experience behind me, I have learned how critical it is to both acknowledge and face your dark side and insecurities, which we all have. One of our most difficult jobs is to learn how to manage those dark feelings when they surface. Our mind is just as powerful as our bodies and it has to be part of our determination and our manifesting. If you believe in yourself, you put yourself where you need to be regardless of the circumstances. So, if I want to be larger than life then I have to act and put myself there. I also have to believe I belong there. I now want to be led by the spirit to take every risk possible taking those leaps into new horizons.

My dream was not to be famous with *Off the Curb*. It was my dream to bring the kids out into the world as far as I could. We performed in Canada, Portugal, Italy, throughout the United States, appeared on the Public Broadcasting Channel, the Black Entertainment Television Station, and opened concerts. I wanted to take my troupe into the world as best as I could given my strengths and my weaknesses. Presently, I am ready to take another leap. I want to embark on a healing journey to share my stories, self-care techniques, and the practices I have developed. I would love to be able to go out in the world and inspire people with motivational talks on how to become their healthiest selves. I have interviewed inspirational individuals as well as given lectures about mind, body, and spirit both to in person audiences and through various media channels. But, I would like to incorporate all of my work- fitness, dance and mental health counseling into become a catalyst in the critical space of mind, body, and spirit development so very needed in today's culture.

Along with implementing my dream to improve the state of humanity, I want financial abundance. I never considered becoming rich as a necessary guarantee for happiness and I still do not. But, I have realized that having financial success is a goal I should consider important to my life. It sets you free to do those things you wish to do without being encumbered by the stresses that most individuals face in managing their routine budgets. I want the freedom to travel the world, to help my friends and family through tough times if necessary, and to partake in life's adventures and luxuries as they present themselves to me. I have worked hard and the work I do is heartfelt, creative, healing, and inspirational and I finally understand the financial value of it. It is important to know my value and essential to receive compensation for my worth. I want my life to reflect the progress that my clients achieve, based on how difficult the work is with which I help them and the expertise required in delivering those skills. I believe it is possible to have financial freedom and to live your dream with abundance in health, in love, and in happy relationships. Having abundance means opening up your spirit to have all that you want including love, health, wealth and joy. There was a time that I felt I did not deserve all that I wanted. I thought that money was not important because I was doing what I wanted to do, but money is an important commodity in my life. As I said, it can set you free. Or conversely it can hold you back. I have the ability to be a role model for other people who are following their dreams, and at the same time can encourage them to believe that they do not have to live in scarcity.

Guidance:

Self-reflection goes back to examining your core beliefs. I had an underlying belief that I did not deserve all that I wanted. Financial abundance was not a priority in my world. I was not brought up in an affluent family. We were brought up to be kind and polite. We were encouraged to have jobs, even at a young age, but not brought up to see ourselves as going above and beyond the scope of middle-class comfort. The idea to become rich and have the means to travel the world and participate in other activities associated with the wealthy was not a goal toward which we were encouraged to attain. Financial security was not a significant core belief for me. Stepping into my own space and allowing myself to become bigger also were not significant core beliefs.

If an individual does experience scarcity in their lives in love, romance, monetary things, business, and friendships they might want to explore their core beliefs and see what is blocking them. Specifically, the question they should consider asking themselves is: What kind of emotional or spiritual block is operating so that you do not receive that which you desire? It may be prudent to work with a therapist who will guide you to figure out where those core beliefs started, and then to learn how to shift your thinking to live a more fulfilling life. There is no reason why every person cannot have everything that they want. It is an ideal to which all of humanity is entitled.

It is possible to have everything that you want in a broad sense. When you are manifesting dreams and visions you do not want to be too specific. Some people think, "Imagine it and it will appear." That of course, is wishful thinking. Manifestation is not magic in the logical sense of the word, perhaps on the ethereal sense of it. A person has to act and place him or herself where the change or goal desired has the fertile ground to develop. If you want to be a dancer in New York City, you have to go there. Manifesting is taking steps to move yourself toward your goal, like googling available jobs, creating appropriate professional relationships, and placing yourself in your desired location. When all is said and done, the hardest concept of all is to trust the universe to do the rest. It may not happen in your time frame but staying on your path will hopefully get you to your desired goal.

In general, most individuals are not familiar with the concept of core beliefs and unless they have had the circumstances to delve into them, the concept is foreign. Most people can understand and recognize that they become the adults they are, as a result of the parents or caretakers who have raised them. However, as babies and children we are all recipients of intrinsic learning, no matter where we have come from or who our caretakers have been.

The child watches the care-giver in the home and the interactions among the people around the home, listening and seeing all that occurs. Certainly, the environment is full of sensory stimuli happening throughout each hour of every day. The child takes in ideas of what the family displays and draws conclusions about what the family should be as the child grows and matures. Those become the core beliefs and the child internalizes them. The beliefs are not necessarily taught per se. Someone doesn't tell you are always going to be lower middle class and you are going to struggle. Rather, the process occurs subconsciously. So too, depending on the dynamics of a given family, opinions and directives are verbalized and repeated and they become part of the core belief system. What you observe and experience at a young age becomes your "normal." You don't realize that there is more. The mindset is established and most individuals mosey through life with those messages internally planted without reason to stop, reflect, or question, unless confronted with negative feelings or an inability to function productively. You go through life and you perpetuate a mindset because that is what you intrinsically learned as a child. It is when you get to adulthood that there is an energetic hold that is stopping you from believing that you deserve more, that you may have a limiting core belief. The opportunities come your way and you don't take them. That core belief has you stuck in an unswerving pattern and can result in feelings of unworthiness.

In addition to taking the time and effort to focus on your own underlying issues, a person must also learn to accept those individuals who choose not to explore their core beliefs and issues. Sometimes those people are close, either family members, friends, partners, and others with whom you have had relationships. It is no easy task to address or accept this reality. The unfortunate truth is that you have to believe in your own strength. That is, you must use your skills and courage to know when it is time to move on and away from those who may be toxic or negative influences. All sorts of resources exist to deal with the multitude of obstacles ingrained or thrown at you, if you choose to rise above them and to live a better life, to choose happiness over stagnation. Depending on the severity of your own resistance to change or moving on, a good counselor or skilled therapist may be necessary. You have the right to interview such a professional to assess whether their style fits with your needs and you should take the time to do this. Your mental health is as important, if not more, as the health of your body. Many individuals will take much time to receive an accurate diagnosis about a medical problem with a physician that they feel comfortable, so why is the same not true for a professional helping you to deal with mental stresses and concerns?

If you choose counseling or therapy and you feel comfortable speaking and working with the person, either long or short term, you must be willing to put into practice the techniques, methods, or tools suggested or determined by this person. Oftentimes, the initial venture into the world of self- exploration is taken on with confidence and zeal. Too frequently as that energy becomes rote, a person can tend to wane away from the hard work of it all and that is truly unfortunate. Because most likely, it is at those times that persistence is needed the most and will become the most helpful. So, going into therapy should be taken on with a firm commitment to leave it eventually with the knowledge that you completed some very hard work. The point is, the level of your progress is directly related to the level of your eventual comfort of being in your own skin. This does not mean that each day of your life will become blissful. It means that you will have gained some skills to manage the days that are difficult and disconcerting.

There is also a grim truth that some individuals do not want to open the Pandora's box of pain because it can uncover a dark place, which is a place they would prefer to leave buried and untouched. Eventually, the pain will emerge in other ways and keep affecting their lives. Those individuals may never feel completely fulfilled or whole. Some people are fine with that. They would rather live less reflectively and remain less self-aware than travel to those painful parts of the soul to do this deep healing work.

Chapter 11 - "Out of the Comfort Zone"

A ship in port is safe;
But that is not what ships are built for.

John A. Shedd

A friend once told me, "You are easy on the soul" and those words made a lasting imprint. Shortly after that conversation, I discovered Tony Robbins. His work speaks to the six basic needs that every person requires. They are: certainty, variety, significance, connection and love, spiritual growth, and contribution. He conducts seminars and workshops to teach those who are interested how to better themselves and move toward a more fulfilling life. His work inspired me to the point that I decided to pursue working as a life coach and to assist individuals in becoming unstuck both personally and professionally. His work had a direct influence on me and life-coaching resonated with my soul.

I decided to return to school and train as a therapist and through my training I deepened as a person. I was exposed to countless spiritual thinkers and extraordinary teachers who taught me a number of therapeutic techniques and self-care tools to educate my clients. I found my new role as a therapist to be an easy fit in my work with physical fitness, dance, and performance. There should exist a healthy interchange between body, soul, and mind because they are all connected to one another. How well we manage our physical bodies and how well functioning they are, directly affects our mental health. Our brains are housed in that body. If our bodies are not healthy and efficient, then our brains will respond in unhealthy and inefficient ways. Whatever you put in your body you are putting into your brain. The opposite is true. Whatever you put into your brain, the body will respond. The inner voice of your brain affects the functioning of your body. If you are surrounded by negative energy or listening to a constant barrage of disturbing news than your body will respond to what your brain is thinking. If you are carrying lots of stress, your body will be affected. Fear and anxiety are direct disturbances to your physical health and especially the nervous system.

I realized that I am able to meet with people and hear their deepest secrets, thoughts, and feelings. I have the capacity to help those in need to work toward a healing self. I was innately born with the desire to help others. This skill has taken me on a number of paths. Some of those I am reiterating from past chapters. The reason for this is to specifically identify the interconnectedness of my work with physical fitness and dance to that of mental fitness and the importance of this meshing. Through my business, MIST (Muscle Integrated Soul Training), I offer personal development including Soul Fitness classes, where I bring to my members those skills and tools I have learned, so they can incorporate them into their own lives. In all programs and classes that I offer, I provide opportunities for participants to move out of their comfort zones. I define this process as moving away from what is familiar, comfortable, and easy. It is making your perspective larger and taking risks. It is becoming adventurous and trying new things and becoming the fullest version of yourself, instead of the comfortable version of yourself. Interestingly, some individuals do not see the value in understanding their spiritual side because they consider themselves just fine. They do not realize that there is a whole other layer they can deepen into, to learn about themselves on a soul level and live a fuller life by trying something that may raise their level of discomfort. I offer people opportunities to perform. Although the participants may not be consciously aware, these experiences bring forth energetic healing and build positive community interactions. These works have included (from most recent):

A Quarantine Flash Mob- A Dance I created while we were in quarantine that was taught virtually and was performed at a community gathering once regulations were partially lifted. Participants were socially distanced and wore masks.

Diversity and Inclusion- This was a Performance showcasing inclusion and diversity that was held at the local high school that included a presentation and discussion around prejudice and personal biases.

Rise Up- A performance for a fundraiser for a young woman battling cancer. She chose the song.

Thriller- A yearly tradition of Michael Jackson's famous song performed around Halloween.

Dancing through the Decades- A choreographed dance piece including all genres such as swing, disco, hip-hop, and pop.

Wedding Proposal Flash Mob- A celebration of a special moment in the life of a couple. I was hired to create this unique performance that led to a wedding proposal.

90s Hip-Hop Medley- A performance held locally as part of a Pride celebration.

Learn to Let Go- A performance created to uplift the community during the quarantine which was displayed on Facebook.

Women in Unity- A video created to encourage empowerment of women. A presentation about "Taking Up Space" followed the showing of the video at the Jane Pickens' Theater in Newport, RI.

My motivation and inspiration to create such events proceeds from the belief that we need more joy and togetherness in our world. We need to get out of our own heads and do things for others that will bring them happiness. I also want to brand my business as a happy energetic place where the members create a harmonious camaraderie, while developing both physically and emotionally.

It is interesting for me to look back at all the times I shrunk to situations. Sometimes the person who gives the advice needs to take their own advice and frankly this is something I strive for at all times. My essence was to be larger than life and I knew there was a world out there waiting for me. I always knew there was more. I wanted and still want to explore the world even though my core beliefs kept me outside the realm of fame. On the other hand, during the *Off the Curb* time period I could get the kids to dance larger than life. I always tried to pull out of the kids from both dancing and from their human sides their best selves. I wanted the dancers to go full out and use every part of themselves when performing. I worked hard to make them believe that they had the ability to be better people and better performers and that it was their responsibility to be the best they could. I continue to convey this message to the members who attend my studio. I encourage them to dig down and dance harder, try heavier weights, and be consistent with their workout schedules and routines. I want them to be dedicated to their bodies and personal developments, to become the best physical, spiritual, and emotional versions of themselves.

I must say my eyes have been opened about how people view my professional persona and feel in my presence. From a positive perspective, I have mentioned how I have been told that I am "easy on the soul" and a "sensei" when teaching. But I have also been told that "some people love Jackie and some people hate Jackie." First, how do I acknowledge that I am not for everyone? There is something about my soul and presence that makes some people feel vulnerable. I learned I have an energy that I did not even realize, although I am becoming much more aware of it now. Some tend to run from this type of energy, while others are drawn to it. Those who run may think I see something in them that they do not want to be seen. It is not spoken about, just an energetic exchange and they turn away. They view me and think of me as a "show off" or "cocky" or "all that" greater than everybody else. I view those people as insecure and unable or unwilling to understand who I am. Why should I be hated? I have not done anything to anyone. What is it about me that they do not like? Maybe they have heard lies or stories or they made up ideas about me. What they have not done is to sit with me to get to know me. I know I am not alone with these types of feelings and questions. Most everyone at some point in their lives has experienced this sort of ostracism. If you have been well-known for a talent or purpose, it is sometimes easy to also become a target. Perhaps, my performance persona becomes confused with my "human" persona. Bottom line, it is easy to falsely judge others from your own insecurities.

People who want more, to evolve, to change and grow find me easy to be around.

They feel it is time to step out of their comfort zones. For people who are safe in their comfort zone and do not want anyone to rock the boat, then I am not so safe to be around. Not everyone feels the need to move away from what is familiar. When they are willing to leave, usually

they have hit rock bottom and feel enough is enough. They cannot tolerate their life situation anymore and want a different and better life. There are those who have an internal longing or nudging, knowing there is more out there and they want to go and find it. In my work, I choose to communicate that there is always a space for hope. I understand that there are those who do not want to heal and remain comfortable in their hopelessness. It takes lots of work and discomfort to make positive changes.

I have been in the business of creating a variety of dance projects involving women who currently attend my classes, who have attended them in the past, or for those who love to dance and perform. When not performing before a live audience, I schedule pop-up performances in the studio for dancers to enjoy the thrill of choreographed dances among a group of like-minded peers. I also create short snippets of a dance routine to be displayed on social media. Those snippets are meant to bring joy to the viewers as well as entice individuals to join the studio. I instruct Cardio Dance classes in my studio as an excellent method of exercise which most participants find enjoyable. What I have found extraordinarily interesting is the dynamic involved with the artform of dance both in the studio and out. The women I work with for the various projects I have created and within the dance classes I teach are sincerely excited to use dance as an expression of themselves as well as for physical fitness. They have established a positive communal feeling, which I encourage and support. In any artform the degree of expertise will vary. My goal is always to encourage the participants to enjoy dancing and resist the temptation to measure their skills against those who have been dancing for a number of years. I am more demanding for on-stage performances rehearsing for precision and excellence to bring the best to viewing audiences. Yet, I am constantly taken aback to see the insecurities of grown women who hesitate to leave their comfort zones. They want to enjoy the class or production, but some allow what they perceive as their imperfections to interfere, which then shakes their ability to move at their best. It is like a self-fulfilling prophesy. In productions, as well as in class to some degree, they want to be perfect. They do not want to be vulnerable. During rehearsals, some women have fun trying to get the steps of the choreography. Others become angry when they cannot master the steps and want to storm off, disappointed in their ability. Both extremes are ever-present. There are women who support each other, help one another, and are so amazingly positive. Other women shrink. When a person has a low self-esteem that person tends to separate from other people. She makes herself smaller. That's what happens for some. They do not dance full out. They shrink. They do not take up space.

For the *Women in Unity* project the theme was to empower women to take up space. For those whose insecurities were getting the best of them, I found I had to intervene with the group. This whole project was to inspire women to step out of their comfort zones and to show who they were. And if the role models in the video were shrinking, they were not going to be role modeling the right message. So, I had to inspire them to step into their power and really own what they were doing. I was surprised that middle aged women still needed this type of encouragement at this point in their lives. What I found I needed to do and continue to do is to bring everything to the next level. That is, to model for women the moves which I repeatedly break down into workable components, while smiling and continually encouraging them to see the beauty within themselves. Each person will come to a dance class or performance with their own unique and individual style in response to the music and the choreography. That process is the beauty of the artform.

The *Women in Unity Project* incorporated a lecture, which was more of a conversation, with time allotted for questions and comments from the audience as well as a final activity for audience participation. Although the video highlighted the power of women, the lecture topic was not exclusive to women. Instead the topic was a universal theme about the inner critics that live inside all individuals. It is the inner voice that we all hear, the voice that holds our fears and inhibitions and stops us in our tracks. It tells us we are not good enough or not strong enough or not courageous enough. That voice most often has its origins from our early childhoods and gains a power of its own for various reasons. If we do not learn how to subdue this voice, it will continually interfere with our ability to function toward the goals we wish to pursue. The character Arya Stark from *The Game of Thrones* served as my example of a powerful woman in leadership who stood up to take her power back with two simple words, "not today." In the series, she moved from being a willful child, yet at times confused, to becoming a force to be reckoned with. And in voicing those two words she made it absolutely clear that no one would sever her power for that moment. Those power moments multiply as an individual assumes control over the inner voice that threatens to sustain the negativity. It speaks to the importance that all individuals need to find compassion for themselves, to learn to quiet that inner negative voice, and to allow the empowered voice that seeks to create, discover, and enjoy life to find its place. Again, the conversation was meant to be all inclusive without diminishing the value of either gender. Women hold life within them, the future beings of the world. How powerful a job is that? We all have the opportunity to take our space and proclaim our power to accomplish all that we desire. At the conclusion of my talk, I asked the audience members to stand and take up their space showing their strength and belief in themselves. I guided them to assume a power stance, arms outstretched and making lots of cheering noises. That stance (with the cheers) can be considered a metaphor for all of my work that binds mind, body, and soul together. I like to focus on my successes as I look back from the highs and lows that brought me where I am today. I'm not a worldwide famous thinker, spiritual leader, performer, physical fitness trainer, counselor, or business woman. Yet, I have functioned in all of those roles as an ordinary person, admired and well-respected by a certain group of individuals, who I like to believe that I have helped or inspired or both.

The Take-Away:

This final chapter has me thinking a variety of thoughts. Through my therapy practice I have seen how joy can be one of the scariest emotions. Those who have suffered deep pain after having had joy in their lives are hesitant to give joy another chance for fear it will once again be taken from them. This is a huge hurdle to overcome. Still others need to move at their own pace with the hope that they can find happiness. Certainly, there are others who simply do not have the capacity to change and consider the world to be a fearful and hopeless place and thrive in that mindset. I will always ascribe to the belief that there is no finish line for emotional healing and there will always be challenges to overcome and lessons to be learned.

What I have learned as a result of my experiences in teaching dance exercise classes, while facilitating performances, is that dance goes hand in hand with performance. The various performances that I create shift with who is performing. I love giving the average person a chance to perform and opening the platform to whoever wants to try. This allows the participants opportunities to leave their comfort zones to try something new, bringing joy to each other and audiences. The performances provide for both in person and social media community interactions.

Success is a hard concept to universally define. Intrinsic to it is embracing failure as a key component in reaching your own personally defined notion of success. Success involves a hard-earned journey, with all sorts of self-reflection and struggles. The hope is always that we comprehend that in being human, we must accept our imperfections and the dark side of our being (the shadow side) that resides within us and all of humanity. To acknowledge those attributes takes much courage, energy, and exploration. We must be willing to become curious about why we make the choices we make and search for where that haunting inner voice developed while learning how to take control of it. Those destructive messages can be tamed with hard work and a willingness to allow them space to reconcile disturbing chatter with healthy thoughts.

It is complicated for individuals to understand and accept that showing our flaws is okay. If you never leave your comfort zone, then you will never learn anything new and possibly never evolve into the person you were meant to be. Both women and men have been judged on their body images and succumb to enhancement treatments or use artificial filters to display themselves on social media. They feel pressured to fulfill some sort of beauty image that is unrealistic. No one can sustain a perfect persona. I have also noticed that there are those who feel as if they are being looked at and judged, when in reality they are self-judging themselves. These individuals have fragile egos and tend to want to hide, especially in class, instead of looking at the skilled and experienced dancers as inspiration to aspire towards. Most people do not care about evaluating those around them and are focused on their own actions. An important take-away from the experiences of the performances and the classes I teach, is the need for individuals to develop resiliency as well as playfulness. None of us is for everyone. And that is perfectly fine. Going into something new and leaving your comfort zone is going to be a little scary until you feel comfortable and get used to the new adventure. You may actually have fun.

Guidance:

If you love an activity, hobby, or artform, never allow anyone to take that love away from you by dissuading, judging, or imposing their will on you to do something different. And by all means, be patient and open-minded with yourself to allocate time to learn that which you want to learn. You will not be perfect the first time you try something. It is important to embrace who you are and accept your flaws and talents. If you allow people to criticize you and anticipate judgement, then you will shut down and become immobilized. Take the leap of faith and follow your heart and passion with your creations. If you want to be a working actor, then you have to act and get paid for it and then you are a working actor. Whoopie Goldberg states, "…be an actor because you love to act. Don't be an actor because you think you're going to be famous, because that's luck." Feed your passion. Do what you love. If timing and luck are on your side, fame may be yours. But the passion and love have to be in the work, not in the outcome.

The *Women in Unity* project was a means to showcase women but some women involved in the project worried about who was actually going to see it. They wanted to make sure they looked their best before the video was shown. As a society we are still feeding an emptiness that comes deep within an individual's soul. For some, there is a void that they are trying to fill by enhancing or changing their physical appearance. Society has imposed this idea of being liked by everyone. Social media has reinforced this idea by encouraging the most "likes" on Instagram and Facebook. We use filters for selfies to disguise our natural appearance and assume a persona like someone on a magazine cover who has been photoshopped. We add eyelashes to make our existing ones look fuller, and use hair extensions to cover up thinning hair. We have become so accustomed to these accentuating features that they have become normalized. This is not to say that individuals cannot have fun "dressing up" and using the enhancements that are available. The problem is when an individual must have these embellishments to validate their existence. In other words, if your self-esteem is so low that your validation comes from others and from a virtual reality then you are never going to have internal peace, happiness, and joy. You have to find within yourself your own joy and self-acceptance. Physical enhancements to your body are not going to make you feel better if you have not internalized self-love. There are lots of walking wounded individuals in the world. The outer shell is temporary so doing soul work brings life-long fulfillment.

 The behaviors exhibited by grown adults, especially the women to whom I have referred is to shy away from engaging in activities like dance with their full heart or they retreat from a group because of their own self-judgements. If you have been raised in a pessimistic environment, your mind has been conditioned to hear negativity and it is hard to believe anything different. Those issues are best addressed through counseling and/or therapy. Unfortunately, our society persists in considering mental fitness as something of a taboo and many individuals avoid it, even when they know intellectually and instinctively that it would be helpful. Often, it is painful going inward and many do not want to be reminded of the past. It is far easier to self-medicate, ignore the pain, or stay in what is familiar than do the work towards healing. Most people need a major life challenge or hit rock bottom to change their lives. I am happy that I have always been a person who is willing to learn, and therefore can impart my lessons to others with authenticity.

As parents and caretakers, we are the primary teachers and role-models for our children. We hope to project confidence and appropriate self-love practices while understanding that we are not perfect and that we will make mistakes. We need to be mindful of how we deal with our own mistakes, our anger, and how we resolve our problems. Our children are little analytical magnets absorbing all that they see, hear, and feel. With our behavioral reactions we are teaching resiliency or the lack of it. Any person in a leadership role in our institutions- schools, churches, activity centers, or athletic fields has the responsibility to be an appropriate role-model to the children in their care. They provide critical support to parents and primary caretakers whether they want that duty or not. However, one of the most difficult aspects of parenting that never ceases is understanding and accepting our children for who they are, their perspectives on life, as well as their true interests. Finding the balance of when and if to intervene for a given situation is the never-ending challenge no matter how old they get. Giving them the freedom to make their own mistakes and to learn from them is yet another parental challenge.

Thoughts to contemplate:
- A person will only change when they are ready.
- We are responsible for taking care of our own spirits, souls, minds, and hearts
- If we put our happiness in the hands of somebody else then we are always going to be hurt

- If you're relying on the virtual world for information, you may not be receiving the whole truth
- We need to talk to people directly to get to know them
- Creating our own narratives through social media and finding only those people who will support that belief system is not healthy
- We have the right to be who we want and to explore interests wholeheartedly without limiting our choices based on what others think or believe
- We need to carry ourselves with confidence and self-assurance and over time those feelings will grow and attract positive energy and individuals

Speaking up is an example of taking your power. The work I do is to always uplift and empower individuals. I realize that for some it is difficult to "rock the boat" and to face those who want to intimidate. The hope is that all individuals can speak up and not tolerate the judgements and harshness of some. Be patient with yourself as you practice these tools. Small steps are better than no steps at all. We must strive to be authentic and see ourselves as kind, reasonable people, with our own set of flaws and weaknesses. Let's quiet the inner critic. Have the courage to sail your ship outside the harbor.

Part Four

Resources

Resources for Chapter 1 - "My Father's Suicide"

I mentioned that I visited a medium for assistance in guiding me through the healing process. And for those that may not be familiar with what a medium is, I present a brief overview. A medium usually channels the energies of people who have passed on to the person who has a session with him or her. They sometimes have psychic abilities. Mediums are all different. The medium I visited channeled energy from angels from whom she receives messages. The work of the medium has to do with the energy that comes to her when willing participants engage in a session with her. A good analogy is to think about twins and how they can feel each other's pain even when they may be in two separate parts of the country. That is a life energy between them. All beings are connected somehow by an energetic force. Whether someone has passed on or not their spirit and energy still exist. For this reason, it was important to me to visit a medium because I had a lot of questions for my father like anyone would from a person who killed himself. I believed the medium could channel my father's energy so I could get answers, and I wanted some healing around this. On this visit, I invited my mother to join me. The medium opened up by identifying that there were angels in the room and they were there to protect us and to keep us safe. She shared different visions of my childhood of me with my father and they were all things that were true in my life. His energy came into the room because both my mother and I wanted it and were open to it. My father wanted to get a message to us. That was a really important part of the healing process-to understand and know why this was his choice. He wanted to let us know that he was close by, that his spirit was still alive, and that his presence was still around us. He was not bones in a grave but rather a spirit there healing and soothing us. I would have to say that for my mother and I, visiting the medium when we did which was years after my father died, was an important step toward my healing process. I understand visiting a medium is not for everyone. I do speak with more specifics about the experience in a future chapter.

    I spoke about attending a grief group as an option for those attempting to explore their sadness as well as other emotions associated with loss. But I believe that one should have some healing time between the passing of a loved one and participating in a grief group. The initial passing of a loved one is shocking and traumatic and to begin the difficult work around healing requires you to be in a sturdier mental state in order to have the ability to share with others. Going too soon can have the opposite effect on a person. Rather than finding consolation and peace, attending too soon can raise anxiety levels and increase one's anger and depression. You have to be willing to share, and also be willing to listen compassionately to what other people share. Sometimes individuals think their loss is so much more intense than another's loss. There should never be a comparison of loss. A grief group is for support and knowing that you're not alone in this process. It's not going to bring the person back. It is being on the same page as others, hearing their loss, and sharing similar feelings of the grieving process with them. A facilitator guiding the process who is well-informed, trained and has the ability to see where everyone is at is an absolute must. Realistically, it may take time to find the right group for the best results. I know participating in a grief group (I found a group for suicide survivors) gave me lots of valuable coping tools and assisted me in healing.

I recommend the books that follow which I found to be comforting and healing and one movie I found to be interesting.

Books:
A Time to Grieve: Meditations for Healing after the Death of a Loved one by Carol Staudacher
Faith in the Valley: Lessons for Women on the Journey to Peace by Iyania Vanzant
A Return to Love by Marianne Williamson

Movie:
The Things We Lost in a Fire- This is perhaps an unusual choice but I felt the story of the pain experienced by an addict overcoming his addiction parallels overcoming the pain of grief.

Resources for Chapter 2
"Solo-Soul"

There are millions of books on raising children and still there is no one definitive manual on how to successfully raise a child. It is so incredibly personal and dependent upon the type of person you are, and all that encompasses your history, culture, and traditions. You must always self-reflect and ensure that you are seeing your child or children as a person or people separate from yourself. Then guide them to develop and grow using their own internal resources and energy.

Brooke Hampton, an author who writes about child-rearing and living a lifestyle close to nature says, "Speak to your children as if they are the wisest, kindest, most beautiful and magical humans on earth, for what they believe is what they will become." She has an interesting view of parenting that is akin to my core belief. Summarizing this belief in its briefest form is to allow children the freedom to explore their interests, and to trust that they will reach their individual conclusions about what is right for them. This does not mean that the parent/s are absent and let their children roam about aimlessly. Quite the contrary. However, the parent/s should strive to abstain from imposing their will on their children regarding what they think children should be or do even when their beliefs collide with your own.

Some suggested reads:
Holy Flow Parenting Facebook Page
BOLD-Blog on Learning and Development- "What Kind of Parent Are you?"
Harry Harkins and the Nature of Affection by Kendra Cherry

Resources for Chapter 3 - "Mother-Daughter"

All relationships hold a degree of complexity and require reflection to be fully understood and meaningful. Mother and daughter relationships can be very complicated and not easily sorted out. However, the most important relationship to understand as an adult is your relationship with yourself, even if on the surface it sounds somewhat selfish. A young child cannot be expected to self-reflect without the guidance of an adult and deserves to be raised by caregivers who are confident enough to face their fallibilities.

A starting off point for adults to explore reasonable tools and insights into their own questions about child-rearing is making use of on-line resources. Virtual learning has become an extremely healthy tool in guiding one to find the information most relevant to an individual's situation while listening to podcasts and/or reading relevant articles and other literature. Karen C. L. Anderson (Author of *Difficult Mothers, Adult Daughters*) has done lots of work on life coaching. Specifically, she has developed methods in how to deal with coming to terms with difficult relationships. Her approach is not to focus on the difficult person alone, but to look inward and understand how your actions play into the dynamic. Most individuals prefer to simply acknowledge the negativity in others as opposed to identifying the triggers within that cause us to react. Understanding these interactions helps us plan ahead mentally and emotionally to become less reactive and more proactive, which may at times mean to remain silent.

It is always helpful to feed your soul with the activities and outlets that bring you joy and peace from meditation practices to exercise to using artistic skills. Conversations with loving friends who listen to you and hear your concerns can help you define those behaviors you have control over and those you do not. Also, giving yourself positive messages and affirmations to silence the inner critic, even if for a short period of time, is a helpful functional life tool. For me, I knew I had much love to give and when I was ready to have a child, my love poured from me to my child with an ease and an emotion which I profoundly respect and appreciate to this day.

I have two books that I would highly recommend. The first is Brene' Brown's *The Gift of Imperfection*, which allows us to acknowledge our imperfections and know that we will make mistakes. It is from our mistakes that we learn about our own vulnerabilities and hence become better acquainted with ourselves.

The second book is Clarissa Pinkola Estes' *Women Who Run with the Wolves: Myths and Stories of the Wild Woman Archetype*. At one point there is a description of how a mother wolf takes her mature pups and frees them into the wild. This is after she has been careful to protect her pups from predators while feeding and nurturing them. She remains in the background as they find their way and later releases them, never knowing if she will see them again. This concept helped me in raising my son. I did everything I could to nurture him to become disciplined, and guided him to thrive as a kind, compassionate, hardworking, independent, and loving man. I make the effort to spend time with him as he does with me. At the same time, I accept his independence. I completed my job the best way I could.

Resources for Chapter 4 - "The Men"

Many valuable resources exist for individuals who wish to explore how the impact of their relationships with primary caretakers affected their ability to choose a loving and positive partner. One excellent source to begin with in order to gain comprehensive information on this topic as well as many other mental health issues is www.helpguide.org. This source offers information that is easily understood, pragmatic, and can be helpful in leading individuals to other appropriate sites or professionals.

Much research over the past four decades about the importance of an infant's attachment to their primary caretaker has found that this one indicator (attachment) is responsible for:

- Shaping the success or failure of future intimate relationships
- The ability to maintain emotional balance
- The ability to enjoy being our authentic selves and to find satisfaction in being with others
- Resiliency- The ability to rebound from disappointment, discouragement, and misfortune

It is extraordinarily difficult work to become introspective and address negative patterns of behavior that are not satisfactory and bring us no joy, but instead hinder our ability to move forward in a productive manner. The difficulty stems from childhood as we grow and develop within our environments and with our primary caretaker/s, our core beliefs which are established by virtue of how we are related to both verbally and non-verbally. Those core beliefs drive us in our subconscious decision making and problem solving. If those mechanisms are not as healthy as we would like, then we have to find a way to reverse them. They will not reverse by magic. It requires lots of effort. All individuals can reap the benefits of good counseling, a skilled therapist, and /or appropriate classes or groups, and the ability to self-reflect.

Other resources to understand the pain from childhood wounds are: *The Power of Now* by Eckhart Tolle- encourages the reader "to become an active observer of your emotional state."

Eckhart Tolle also provides podcasts on his teachings through YouTube.

The Body Keeps the Score: Brain, Mind, and Body in the Healing of Trauma by Bessel van der Kolk- deeply explores the effects of trauma on an individual and subsequent effects on society and professes, "Social support is not the same as merely being in the presence of others. The critical issue is *reciprocity* being truly heard and seen by the people around us, feeling that we are held in someone else's mind and heart."

Rainbow in the Cloud: The Wisdom and Spirit of Maya Angelou- This is an inspirational collection of Maya Angelou's many words of wisdom and can be turned to for comfort, spiritual guidance, laughter, and profound understanding.

It is always important to return to self-care practices when attempting to use resources to self-reflect and improve the quality of our lives. Sometimes the simplest of activities help to relieve stress, anxiety, and self -criticism that originates from the deep-seated wounds of our past. So:

- First, be kind to yourself, and give yourself a break from over-thinking
- Listen to your instincts and give them space; they are telling you something
- Seek bodywork; specifically, Rolfing
- Consider Reiki principles and practices for healing
- Do not ignore the red flags; know the patterns that you are repeating
- Identify narcissistic and addictive behaviors and how to heal from them
- Have at least one person who tells you the truth

Finally, once we have identified what our negative patterns of behavior are, then we need to put a plan into place to cope with the triggers. We must value ourselves and learn to believe we are worth the best in a partner, a person who will see and hear you for all that you need to say and be. I would recommend Byron Katie's *A Thousand Names for Joy* as a book that guides a person through the process of truly understanding the reality of joy. Thich Nhat Hanh's *Being Peace* is a forever source with which to refer for profound life teachings on your inner life and soul.

Resources for Chapter 5 - "Mother-Son Bond"

I think about helpful resources for Mother-Son bond as falling into a couple of categories. In terms of parenting questions and concerns, there is no one manual for child-rearing while many tried and true experts throughout the years have attempted to guide parents through the various stages of parenting, some more helpful than others. Certainly, the advice is listened to and perhaps adhered to in a number of situations. In the end, common sense, instincts, and conversations with loved ones, spiritual advisors, or other respected individuals are probably the most important resources for parents. There are instances where the professional assistance of a therapist or counselor is required. The hope is that individuals enter the wonderful experience of child-rearing with a positive attitude and loving inclinations. Under any circumstances, I would encourage the individuals to prepare emotionally for the tumultuous ride of joy and sadness as you watch your child deal with the growing pains that we all face throughout our lives. Some things to think about and discuss with others when necessary is how to:

- Help children through trauma

- Establish agreeable family traditions that enhances a child's development and connection to others
- Impart your values and beliefs to your child, knowing theirs may change as they mature
- Maintain open and honest communication with the child as s/he becomes an adult
- Remain flexible, supportive, and understanding during times of conflict
- Enjoy, share, and relish in your child's individuality
- Never compare your child to another as a means to evaluate strengths and weaknesses
- Know that you may not always understand or agree with your child's perspective

With regard to divorce, it does leave its unique effects on the parents and children and cannot be ignored. However, any life-altering event or change in a family will leave its emotional mark as well. The best the adults can do is model for the children healthy coping skills, resiliency, and perspective in adjusting to the complicated future adjustments in life's routines. I also believe that adults need to have time to nurture their individual needs as they embark on this journey of change. Too often, one parent or both, feel guilty and perhaps try to overcompensate in helping their children. Yet, the whole family in their own individual ways have much to do as they move toward healing and time has to be allowed for self-care and comfort. So, parents and children need to use the outlets that bring them peace and joy that may range from sitting quietly to participating in bustling activities.

I present standard guidelines for parents who are divorcing according to Amy Morin, LCSW that are worth contemplating, knowing that the process will not be perfect:
- Co-parent peacefully
- Avoid putting kids in the middle
- Maintain healthy relationships
- Use consistent discipline
- Monitor adolescents closely
- Empower your children with resiliency
- Teach Coping skills
- Help kids feel safe
- Seek Parent Education
- Get Professional help

In general, parents can be extraordinarily hard on themselves, and it is impossible to not bring their own insecurities into the role and responsibility of healthy parenting. Deep love is a must, but the love does not always relieve the doubtfulness or anxiety when evaluating how a given situation was handled. In most cases, the love will be felt by the child and therefore can never be underestimated. It is essential that the child is seen and heard for who s/he is. It is encouraged that parents practice self-forgiveness for not being perfect.

I offer five interesting books suggested by Tess Brigham, a San Francisco-based psychotherapist and certified life-coach who works primarily with millennials and millennial parents.

Peaceful Parent, Happy Kids: How to Stop Yelling and Start Connecting by Laura Markham

Daring Greatly: How the Courage to be Vulnerable Transforms the way We Live, Love, Parent, and Lead by Brene' brown

How to Raise Successful People: Simple Lessons for Radical Results by Esther Wojcicki

Helping Your Anxious Child: A Step-by-Step Guide for Parents by Ronald M. Rapee, Ann Wignall, Susan Spence, Vanessa Cobham, Heidi Lyneham

Permission to Feel: Unlocking the Power of Emotions to help Our Kids, Ourselves, and Our Society Thrive by Marc Brackett

Resources for Chapter 6 - "*Off the Curb*: Its Inception"

    With regard to following through on your creative ideas, I must simply begin by saying follow through on them. Some individuals may have a need to sit and write an organized plan with steps clearly delineated and then check things off as they go along. Others may "shoot from the hip" and allow their instincts to drive them through the process. Still others, may utilize a combination of both methods, or implement a strategy completely out of the box. The point is, a creative person must decide on their own individual best method to bring their ideas to fruition however and with whatever is necessary. It is helpful to consult with those you believe are on the same wavelength and will listen to your vision, while listening to how they achieved their success as well as recognizing the pitfalls they may have encountered.

    Turning to inspirational leaders, thinkers, or artists can offer motivation to help you develop trust in your strength to accomplish your goals. Those individuals are personal to you, your beliefs, and your spirit. It is how you connect to the individual, and what that person offers to you in the way of knowledge and hope. My Holy Trinity is Jesus, Buddha, and Mr. Rogers each for their wisdom and kindness. I studied the Bible in depth at one point in my life and found great understanding in the teachings of Jesus, specifically with the profound love he espoused, and in his professing of resisting judgmental behaviors. Jesus appeared to help humanity deal with all the evil that surrounds us. He came to help us turn to him as a leader wanting humanity to follow the goodness that surrounds us instead of the evil. It is not my intention to advocate the following of an organized and structured religion based on the teachings of Jesus, but rather to see him as a leader for humanity. In a similar fashion, I have used the teachings of Buddha for comfort, for inspiration, and for my spiritual growth. The teachings are simple yet forthright and encourage the individual to learn the benefits of silence and meditation. It is a good practice to clear away the clutter in the mind to bring focus on that which will bring one satisfaction and fulfillment. And in so doing, you become a peaceful individual, emitting goodness throughout society while doing your part to add to the harmony of humanity. I enjoyed Mr. Rogers as a child, the third component of my trinity. As an adult I have really gained an appreciation for his character, his personality and the significance of his messages to both children and adults. His television series encouraged children to use their imaginations to enjoy life. He included famous guests as well as regular people of all backgrounds who shared their talents. And he calmly and compassionately dealt with difficult issues that children may have experienced and provided comfort and understanding with his own unique personality which was sometimes misunderstood.

 I have grown to realize that often times, it is extraordinarily difficult for individuals to take a risk and to leave their comfort zones. This difficulty becomes apparent in the ability to act upon a burning desire for fear of failure, to place yourself in the shoes of another to understand their perspective, and to be open to new and unusual genres in a given art medium. Many individuals are controlled by their fears and insecurities. In the spirit of acceptance, I have also learned you have to let those individuals hold on to those feelings until they are ready to explore other options. Acknowledging that the disparity exists is perhaps the best option for both groups, in reaching for and moving toward a middle ground.

My suggestions for excellent resources are:
The Netflix Series- *Hip-Hop Evolution*, Executive Producers: Russell Peters, Sam Dunn, Nelson George, Scott Mcfadyen
Documentary- *Mr. Rogers: It's You I Like*, Executive Producer: Ellen Doherty

Books:
Change Your Thoughts-Change Your Life, Living the Wisdom of the Tao by Dr. Wayne W. Dyer
The Big Payback, The history of the business of Hip-Hop by Dan Charnas
The Bible

Resources for Chapter 7 -
"*Off the Curb*- Passion for Dance"

It is not enough to say, "follow your passion." You must believe in yourself and surround yourself with those individuals who will help develop your skills. In the dance world, take classes continually from those who can teach you moves that offer you a challenge. Keep yourself in good physical shape to avoid injuries, which will most likely occur from time to time. Attending live performances to analyze techniques and methods are helpful. Watching dance movies, both old and new with an eye toward choreography is inspirational. Immersing yourself in the works of the experts is the starting position from which you will push yourself off into personalizing your own craft and style.

In my situation, I chose two paths. One was to teach fitness and dance classes and the other was to create a dance troupe. In both instances, my love for dance was the motivation and second to this love was my desire to make this passion my vocation. I sought to become the best dancer I could be, the best choreographer, and the best teacher and these skills were developed in a number of ways. I had dance teachers that were inspirational both by their energy and passion and their skills in working with students. In some instances,

I observed how they interacted with difficult or unskilled students. Other times, I watched how they handled the protocols of their classes. I saw how some teachers approached their work with complete jubilance. I took from them what felt right and comfortable for my style and pursued my own methods and techniques that were true to my talent and desires.

When seeking to make your passion your profession I have a few suggestions that you may find helpful:

- Using inspirational outlets are not just limited to the genre in which you are working; other artforms may provide inspiration for backdrops, costumes, or configurations.
- Building community relationships for performance venues and opportunities is essential in gaining exposure and to have the final gratification of live performance.
- Traveling to different states and countries to see similarities and differences in dance compositions and performances can be inspiring while opening avenues for discovery.
- Creating a network that allows for learning the intricacies in the development of a workable dance troupe may involve losing members if behaviors warrant this action.
- Learning how to bring your group to its best possible level may take some time
- Reconciling differences among group members, having the dancers understand your concept and being flexible to take suggestions when appropriate is part of the work
- Seeking outside assistance for finance and business considerations is appropriate when organizing this complicated but manageable component

- Getting to know organizations and leaders in a given community is essential
- Requesting help and coaching is acceptable

I would direct your attention to view or read the following:

Off the Curb Documentary- Located on the MIST website under videos.

Rainbow in the Cloud by Maya Angelou- A very inspirational book of a collection of Angelou's words of wisdom organized by categories meaningful to her, yet universal to all.

To Bless the Space Between Us by John O'Donohue- A book of poetry that is organized around themes that provide comfort and understanding. Each chapter begins with a narrative overview of the theme to be explored in beautiful verses.

Resources for Chapter 8 - *"Off the Curb* – The Power of a Mentor"

I am extraordinarily interested in guiding individuals to find the good in themselves and I believe I have always had that desire. Throughout my work with the *Off the Curb* troupe, I continually found myself in the position with the teens to guide them through their personal issues. I did this not knowing that I was on some sort of spiritual journey, counseling and encouraging them to strive to become the best version of themselves. That version had to be found within, on their own as they grew and matured. I was frequently placed in the position of having to help the students untangle their struggles and problems, outside of the interpersonal conflicts of the dance troupe. Interestingly, my work with *Off the Curb* was the foundation of what I was going to pursue, with more depth later on in my life, which was to earn a Master's Degree in counseling. I should note that when confronted with personal issues that the dancers brought to my attention and were beyond my scope, I did turn to the professional agencies with which I had an association, to gain insight and guidance in following a given direction. It is critical to understand your strengths and your limitations in dealing with an adolescence's life and seeking help is always a viable and productive option. My work was in performance, but quickly evolved into the function of a mentor as well and I took that role very seriously.

Without really knowing it initially, my dancers relied on me as a caring adult to whom they could turn for help and assistance. Once they realized that they had developed trust in me, it became a natural and positive strategy to seek appropriate advice and guidance. The same actions are true with adults. That is, we may not always be consciously aware the we too turn to mentors to help us sort through what our needs and desires may be, which is different than how we turn to our friends. Often, we need professional, creative, business, or any other category of guidance in order to reach a goal we have set for ourselves. The person/s we directly seek, the mentor, has to have certain attributes to provide optimal assistance. A good mentor's attributes may include but are not limited to:

- Expertise in the area to be pursued (Why not seek out the best?)
- An alignment of values and beliefs (If you do not respect their values, why waste time with them?)
- An interest in guiding (Give me an honest assessment and then let me choose if I agree.)
- A commitment in helping to make connections (Who needs a person who will not follow-through?)
- Faith in one's ability, skills, and talents (If you do not believe in my vision, do not give me false hope.)

It is a complicated process in finding and trusting those who can and are willing to assist another person toward their "dreams" but also a humble process when you realize that you may need that help.

Bouncing ideas and plans off of an authentic mentor is most gratifying and beneficial. Many formalized workshops exist in training an individual in the protocols and responsibilities of Mentorship and would be an excellent resource for those interested. Those workshops are subject specific.

The resources I took advantage of for dance varied among a multitude of options. I thoroughly enjoyed the tap dance steps of Gene Kelly as well as watching videos of a myriad of dancers like Michael and Janet Jackson. However, their moves, among others, served as inspiration and I always made my choreography unique and my own. I never used another person's choreography for my performances and made sure to credit those who offered me inspiration. Creative inspiration will come to those from just about any place and venue.

Suggested Resources:
For dance ideas and inspiration-
Culture Shock Dance Center- Owner Angie Bunch, accessed by cultureshockdancecenter.com
dancemagazine.com- Offers a number of articles about all aspects of dance including the community, resources, and technical information.

For Mentoring- *The Mentoring Manual* by Julie Starr- A step by step guide who purports that the job of a mentor is about, "waking someone up to who they really are." The challenge is, "to distill their own experience unto bite-sized chunks of wisdom, help or guidance in ways that ultimately help them discover that."

Jackie Henderson

For self-development- Among the many books out there, *The Power of Now* by Eckhart Tolle is an excellent resource to explore that which is encompassed in finding spiritual enlightenment.

Resources for Chapter 9 - "More Past, Regrets, Relationships"

An outlet of your choice that you truly enjoy is an excellent resource to release negative feelings that may be circulating within your body and mind. Techniques, tools, and practices to consider to calm the nervous system follow:

- Enjoying nature
- Using deep breathing
- Journaling
- Meditation
- Dance
- Music
- Knitting

Getting to the point of finding solace in activities takes some work. You have to be willing to address underlying issues that have interfered with your ability to live in a peaceful and healthy manner. Part of the pathology of mental illness is the resistance to process and feel the pain. Also, as has been very prevalent in current society, mental illness holds a stigma for many individuals which is unfortunate and counter-productive to society as a whole. Many individuals who have been traumatized as children have not been taught how to communicate productively. Instead, if the proper therapeutic techniques and methods could be implemented to assist in recovery, then there can be hope for a shift in one's thinking. The necessary introspection entails all of life's past problems even the most treacherous of those. That is to say, viewing those past incidences as unfortunate occurrences can act as a lesson from which to learn. Much easier said than done. Our natural inclination is to avoid the deep pain with as much energy as possible rather than confront it.

Suggested Books:

Man's Search for Meaning by Viktor E. Frankl- Frankl recounts his experience and survival in concentration camps and his theory of "logotherapy." In essence, it is to find the meaning in one's life. Extraordinary story of resiliency and survival.

Being Peace

In an Unspoken Voice: How the body releases Trauma and Restores Goodness by Peter A. Levine, PhD- The author examines the power of the mind to assist in the healing process of those who have suffered injuries and/or traumatic experiences. He uses human nature, the study of animals in their natural environment, and scientific neurological information.

Podcasts:

Podcasts are a helpful medium to explore issues and to find comfort in the fine art of listening. I would recommend the podcasts of Tony

Robbins who assists in defining personal success and how to get there.

Deepak Chopra provides step by step guidance in meditation as well as exploring the connection between mind and body.

Resources for Chapter 10 - "Manifesting Dreams"

Individuals absolutely have the capacity to change core beliefs. Having the awareness that there is something holding you back, and knowing that you want something more is step one. Accepting this concept, and venturing on the journey to discover the specific belief that is holding you back and exploring its origin is step two. Step three involves the hard work of finding the onset of the core belief, learning how to reframe it, and learning the skills to move past the belief. The work is emotionally challenging and there is no one way to deal with underlying emotional issues. I recommend working with a body-centered therapist who can guide you through understanding how to rid yourself of a belief that no longer serves your best interests. Additionally, or in conjunction with a therapist, a Reiki Master, or a Rolfer can help release pent up negative energies through body and energy work.

A Reiki Master is a body worker who moves your energy that gets stuck in your chakras. A true Reiki Master will feel where your energy is stuck and help you to move the energy. The Reiki Master will give you specific practices to work on, suggest books to read and podcasts to listen to, along with affirmations to recite to keep the energy moving.

A Rolfer is a body worker who moves the fascia in the muscles which is scar tissue. It was created by Ida Rolf and it is a whole system that works through the body to realign and readjust anything that became off balance in life, physically or emotionally. The Rolfer's work helps to shift the body to balance it structurally and emotionally by releasing not only the muscle damage but the emotional energy within the muscle that is held from trauma.

The work toward becoming your best self never stops and takes an inordinate amount of energy and commitment. I would like to encourage you to decide to be optimistic and to visualize that which you would love to see happen for yourself. Develop faith in your abilities and skills and surround yourself by those who will encourage your dreams. Create that circle of support and become a member of the circle for others. Be surrounded by people who encourage your dreams and do not discourage your efforts. Those who will encourage your creativity, who are uplifting for your imagination, your dreams, and goals. If you are comfortable then strive to think outside the box and have the willingness to reach out. There is no one person who can change your own individual world for you. Only you can do this.

A number of inspirational stories and accounts are available that tell the stories of individuals who have undergone extreme difficulties and detail how they overcame them. These individuals are examples of dedicated humans in the world who have proven the adage that, "anything is possible."

Suggested Resources:

Wishes Fulfilled: Mastering the Art of Manifesting by Wayne W. Dyer- This book addresses how one can retrain their mind to imagine and obtain those things they dream about for themselves.

The Secret by Rhonda Byrne- This is a self-help book that promotes the notion of using positive thinking to attract others who will emit positive energy. The idea of gratitude and visualization as a helpful tool is discussed.

Think and Grow Rich by Napoleon Hill initially published in 1937- Hill describes his method for attaining wealth through what he describes as his "secret" available to all who may be interested. He portends that wealth begins with an idea.

You can Heal Your Life by Louise L. Hay- Hay's book helps the reader deal with stress and unhealthy thought patterns. She believes, if we change the way we think we can change the way we live. Hay promotes the use of positive affirmations.

The movie *Heal* Directed by Kelly Noonan- This movie is described as a "scientific and spiritual journey where we discover that by changing one's perceptions, the human body can heal itself."

A Podcast heard on NPR "How I Built this"- Guy Raz recounts stories of innovators, entrepreneurs, and idealists and the companies they built or the movements established.

Any number of Autobiographies with hopeful stories

Using self-care practices:
Enjoying Music
Meditation
Self-talk
Good Nutrition and Exercise

Resources for Chapter 11 - "Out of the Comfort Zone"

I am motivated to use my creativity mostly by "divine inspiration" and ideas that take hold of my spirit. I would encourage all individuals to find their personal truths and use their voices to speak about issues that impact them deeply. This can be accomplished by initiating or participating in creative endeavors that highlight a cause or an idea. Although it may be difficult and/or uncomfortable, I encourage you to not remain silent about any injustice directed against you. Not everyone has the ability to create an artistic piece, but you can always find a way to join in on an event or activity as a means to optimize your power.

Enrolling and participating in classes that stimulate your interest provides a means to interact with others, gain confidence, increase skill levels, find satisfaction and happiness with a sense of community. Each of us has our strengths and weaknesses and a purpose in life to fulfill. That purpose is not always obvious, but it is there and will eventually unveil itself. The hope and goal of participating in hobbies you enjoy is that you embrace your gifts, quiet the inner critic, practice self-compassion and become your authentic self.

There are a number of resources to tap into to inspire, support, prod, and awaken you. I suggest a few resources.

Suggested Books:

Imagine a Woman in Love with Herself by Patricia Lynn Reilly
This book will challenge you to explore the beauty you hold within with meaningful affirmations and helpful exercises of finding peace.

The Essential Rumi Translated by Coleman Barks
A collection of poetry of ghazals (odes) and rubai (quatrains) best described as "food and drink, nourishment for the part that is hungry for what they give. Call it soul."

Videos:

Women in Unity Video- The completed video located on YouTube.
The Full Convo-Take Up Space, Tell Your Critics, "Not Today"- Located on YouTube.

Movie:

The Wrong Missy Directed by Tyler Spindle
A film that is seemingly silly that takes a turn toward an interesting message about the quirky personality of a woman who has a big heart and soul beneath her exterior.

Podcast:

Gary Vee- Gary Vaynerchuck will inspire you with his messages about staying true to who you are and reaching for those goals you wish to achieve by remaining motivated in spite of hindrances and working hard.

A Final Note

In this final note, I am combining my story with take-aways, guidance, and resources as a congealed synopsis of some of my lingering thoughts. My goal for this book is for people to feel empowered in who they are. I enthusiastically encourage you to do a good, solid, and healthy life self-reflection to celebrate your accomplishments. Honor those in your heart who have supported you on your journey. Then take a look at what may be stopping you from reaching your goals. And accept those who have not been supportive. These individuals are meant to teach you other lessons. By remaining authentic about the self-reflection process, we all realize that everyone is not meant to be in our lives. When you stand in your authentic light, you attract people who are meant to be there. We simply do not click with all people.

You need to be for yourself first and foremost and do not have to tolerate anything less. "Self-full" puts you first. This absolutely does not mean that a person should judge, criticize, or rebuke another. It means to accept the fact that all persons do not fit within your energy circle, and you do not fit within theirs. Different groups enjoy and vibe with one another, while others do not. As young children we are taught to be "nice" to everyone. What is lost by this tenet is the belief that children are little souls and are born with their own individual inclinations, and preferences. We should guide our young to be kind, loving, and humane persons, while also recognizing their individuality and autonomy. This establishes the foundation for future healthy adults.

We all have the right to stand up for ourselves, to speak our truths, and use our voices. We must clear out the basement of our emotions, entering the dark parts of our lives to be transparent and see what is working and what is not. This includes figuring out where the pain comes from and facing it. It also includes owning failures and short comings as well. When you create a relationship with yourself and stand proud about who you are, you are going to attract like- minded people. Some people will fall away and those are not your people. It may be lonely if you're on the "road less traveled" doing deep soul- searching work, but you are doing what is right for you. I recognize that self-reflection is difficult work. I understand that many people carry lots of shame that blocks them from developing fulfilling relationships and reaching their goals because they do not feel good enough. I hope my book will inspire and ease those feelings and be a fruitful guide toward a better understanding of how to make this journey.

I say trust in the universe. But what is the universe? It is your body and soul. The two are intrinsically and intuitively connected. The soul is the collective part of the unconscious that houses both wisdom and the inner critic. The body holds the memories that made us feel both joyful and sad. Our bodies know everything that we have experienced. I like to abide by the words, "We are not human beings having a spiritual experience. We are spiritual beings having a human experience" stated by Pierre Teilhard de Chardin. Taking care of our souls in whatever form that takes, is as important as taking care of our physical bodies.

Lastly, creativity comes from within the soul and spirit without a logical explanation. Those who have the desire to create also have a vision of the end result. It is their primary concern to fulfill its completion. A journalist commented to Roy Disney (Walt Disney's brother) upon the opening of the Epcot Theme Park in Florida, "Well, I know it seems like a beautiful day, but it must be bittersweet for you knowing Walt never got to see this."

Roy answered, "Walt saw this. That's why you're seeing it now."

I did not create a "Disney World," but I have had a number of "visions" upon which I successfully acted and never allowed anyone to dissuade me from that which I dreamed. I wish the same for all of you who share my journey as represented in my book, *You are not for Everyone*: *A Soulful Guide to Authentic Living.*

Works Recommended or Consulted

1. *Being Peace* Thich Nhat Hanh, Berkeley: Parallax Press, 1987
   Parallax Press
   P.O. Box 7355
   Berkeley, California 94707
   www.parallax.org
2. *In an Unspoken Voice, How the body releases trauma and restores goodness,*
   Peter A. Levine, PhD, North Atlantic Books, Berkeley, CA, 2010
   North Atlantic Books
   P.O. Box 12327
   Berkeley, California 94712
3. *Taking the Leap, Freeing ourselves from old habits and fears,* Pema Chodron,
   Shambhala Publications, 2009
   Shambhala Publications, Inc.
   Horticultural Hall
   300 Massachusetts Avenue
   Boston, Massachusetts 02115
   www.shambhala.com

4. *The Wild Edge of Sorrow, Rituals of renewal and the sacred work of grief,*
   Francis Weller, North Atlantic Books, Berkeley, CA, 2015
5. *Rainbow in the Cloud, The wisdom and spirit of Maya Angelou,*
   The Estate of Maya Angelou, Random House, 2014
6. *To Bless the Space Between Us,* John O' Donohue, Doubleday, 2008
7. *A Thousand Names for Joy, Living in harmony with the way things are,*
   Byron Katie, Three Rivers press, New York, 2007
8. *Change Your Thoughts, Change Your Life, Living the wisdom of the Tao,*
   Dr. Wayne W. Dyer, Hay House, 2007
9. *Man's Search for Meaning,* Viktor E. Frankl, Beacon Press, Boston, 1959
   Beacon Press
   25 Beacon Street
   Boston, Massachusetts 02108-2892
10. *Grace Unfolding, Psychotherapy in the spirit of the Tao-Te Ching,*
    Greg Johanson and Ron Kurtz, Bell Tower, New York, 1991
11. *Tao Te Ching,* Lao Tzu, Barnes and noble Classics, 1991
    Barnes and Noble Books
    122 Fifth Avenue
    New York, New York 10011

12. *The Essential Rumi,* Translated by Coleman Barks, Harper Collins, 2004
13. "The Natural Warmth of the Heart," Pema Chodron, July 14, 2021 wwwlionsroar.com
14. *Holy Flow Parenting Facebook Page,* "Barefoot Five, Magic in the Making, www.barefootfive.com/holy-flow-parenting
15. "A Psychotherapist Shares the 5 Best Parenting Books for Raising Strong and Confident Kids" February, 27, 2020, Tess Brigham, Contributor@MFTTESS, Tim Roberts
16. "The Psychological Effects of Divorce on Children, take steps to help kids bounce back faster" Amy Morin, LCSW, Medically Reviewed by Joel Forman, MD, Updated on August 6, 2019.
17. "Mothers and Daughters: Building a Healthy Relationship" Diane Barth, *Psychology Today* @fdbarth2019.
18. *Thrive Global- 5 Reasons Why You Need a Mentor*, Thriveglobal.com
19. *A Mind at Home with Itself,* Byron Katie and Steve Mitchell, Harper One, 2017.
20. "Aging and Exercise: What does the Research Say?" Michael J. Joyner, MD. *Aging Well*, Volume 6, Number 1, 2000.
21. *Edge,* "The Social Significance of Rap and Hip-Hop Culture, Becky Blanchard, "Poverty and Prejudice: Media and Race." July, 1999.
22. *Medical News Today,* "Everything you need to know about Reiki," Medically reviewed by Ann Marie Griff O.D.

September 6, 2017. Written by Tim Newman. www.medicalnews.com

23. *The Body Keeps the Score*: *Brain, Mind, and Body in the Healing of Trauma*, Bessel van der Kolk M.D. Penguin Books, 2015.
24. *Imagine a Woman in Love with Herself*, Patricia Lynn Reilly, Conari Press, 1999.
25. *A Time to Grieve*: *Meditations for Healing after the Death of a Loved One*, Carol Staudacher, Harper San Francisco, 1994.
26. *Faith in the Valley*: *Lessons for Women on the Journey to Peace*, Iyania Vanzant, Atria Books, 2001.
27. *A Return to Love*, Marianne Williamson, Harper Collins, 1992.
28. *BOLD-Blog on Learning and Development-* "What Kind of Parent Are You?"
29. *The Gifts of Imperfection,* Brene' Brown, Hazelton, 2010
30. *Women Who Run with the Wolves*: *Myths and Stories of the Wild Woman Archetype,* Clarissa Pinkola Estes, Ballantine Books, 1989.
31. *The Power of Now*, Eckhart Tolle, New World Publishers, 1997.
32. *Peaceful Parent, Happy Kids*: *How to stop yelling and start connecting*, Laura Markham, Tarcher Perigee, 2012.
33. *Daring Greatly*: *How the courage to be vulnerable transforms the way we live, love, parent, and lead,* Brene' Brown, Avery, 2012.

34. *How to Raise Successful People: Simple Lessons for Radical Results*, Esther Wojcicki, Houghton Mifflin Harcourt, 2019.
35. *Helping Your Anxious Child: A Step-by-Step Guide for Parents*, Ronald M. Rapee, Ann Wignall, Susan Spence, Vanessa Cobham, Heidi Lyneham, New Harbinger Publications, 2008.
36. *Permission to Feel: Unlocking the Power of Emotions to Help Our Kids, Ourselves, and Our Society Thrive,* Marc Brackett, Macmillan Publishers, 2019.
37. *The Big Payback, The History of the Business of Hip-Hop*, Dan Charnas, New American Library, 2010
38. *Dancemagazine.com*
39. *The Mentoring Manual*, Julie Starr, Pearson Publications UK, 2014.

Films, Series, Documentaries, Podcasts

1. *The Things We Lost in a Fire*, Susanne Bier- Director, Written by Allan Loeb, 2007.
2. The Netflix Series- *Hip-Hop Evolution*, Executive Producers: Russell Peters, Sam Dunn, Nelson George, Scott Mcfadyen, 2016.
3. Documentary- *Mr. Rogers*: *It's You I Like*, Executive Producer: Ellen Doherty, 2018.
4. *Off the Curb* Documentary, MIST Website
5. Tony Robbins-Podcast
6. Deepak Chopra- Podcast
7. *Women in Unity Video* found on YouTube
8. *The Full Convo -Take Up Space, Tell Your Critics, "Not Today"* found on YouTube
9. *The Wrong Missy* Directed by Tyler Spindle, 2020.
10. Gary Vee Podcasts – Gary Vaynerchuck

Jackie Henderson has dedicated her life to Dance, Fitness, and Mental Health. She lives and works on Aquidneck Island in Rhode Island. She created the *Off the Curb* dance troupe which performed throughout the United States as well as overseas from 1992 until 2008 & continues to teach dance & fitness classes in her studio MIST (Muscle Integrated Soul Training). Jackie is also a licensed holistic mental health counselor in private practice.

The memoir recounts Jackie Henderson's story from her childhood until present describing her many accomplishments while traversing through many challenging times and situations. The readers of this fascinating memoir will leave the book having learned valuable life lessons, access to a number of resources, and insight to explore how to live your best life.

If you loved the book and want to learn how to stop people please, how to live your best life, & and how to set healthy boundaries, book Jackie to coach you on living your best life:
www.mistfitness.com

Made in the USA
Coppell, TX
29 December 2024

43675619R00157